HISTORY'S
TRICKIEST
QUESTIONS

450

Questions That Will Stump, Amuse,
and Surprise

PAUL KUTTNER

Foreword by Joseph F. Kett

AN OWL BOOK / HENRY HOLT AND COMPANY / NEW YORK

Henry Holt and Company, Inc.
Publishers since 1866
115 West 18th Street
New York, New York 10011

Henry Holt® is a registered
trademark of Henry Holt
and Company, Inc.

Published in Canada by Fitzhenry & Whiteside Limited,
91 Granton Drive, Richmond Hill, Ontario L4B 2N5.

Library of Congress Cataloging-in-Publication Data
Kuttner, Paul.
History's trickiest questions: 450 questions that will stump,
amuse, and surprise / Paul Kuttner ; foreword by Joseph F. Kett.—
1st Owl Book ed.
p.   cm.
"An Owl book."
Includes index.
1. History—Miscellanea.   2. Questions and answers.   I. Title.
D21.K957   1992
907.6—dc20   92-5569
CIP
ISBN   0-8050-2127-2 (An Owl Book: pbk.)

Henry Holt books are
available for special
promotions and premiums.
For details contact:
Director, Special Markets.

First published in hardcover by Dawnwood Press in 1991.

First Owl Book Revised and Expanded Edition—1992

Designed by Katy Riegel

Printed in the United States of America
All first editions are printed on acid-free paper.∞

9   10

To the memory of
Margarete and Paul, my parents, and
Annemarie, my sister,
and also to
Stephen, my son,
and to
Ursula Fraenkel and Ilse Jochimsen.

CONTENTS

FOREWORD

Paul Kuttner has written a lively and suggestive book that should stimulate the curiosity of readers about history and related fields. It arrests attention by posing questions that are "tricky" in the sense that they are rarely asked and elicit surprising answers. Readers should not feel embarrassed if they do not know most of the answers, for this book is not designed as a test of core knowledge, or what E. Donald Hirsch, James Trefil, and I have called "cultural literacy." A roomful of historians probably would come up with most of the answers, but an individual historian is likely to know only a fraction. While I happened to know that the famous Civil War encounter between the *Monitor* and the *Merrimack* is misnamed (at the time of the battle the *Merrimack* had been renamed the *Virginia*), it was news to me that Helen Gahagan Douglas called Richard Nixon soft on Communism during their mud brawl for the House of Representatives in 1950 and that most of the weapons sent by the United States to the contras in Nicaragua were manufactured in Communist countries.

And there is more. Readers will learn why Romanians once hailed Dracula as a hero, and they will be introduced to a treasure of interesting information about World War II and the Nazis, including the low comedy surrounding the death of the Nazi "martyr" Horst Wessel. One of the leading features of *History's Trickiest Questions* is that the answers frequently go beyond the questions by providing auxiliary information and connecting threads. Thus a brief question about why the British cut off the funnels of a lend-lease destroyer during World War II leads to a tale of extraordinary British daring, heroism, and plain ruthlessness. Pricking the interest of readers, leading them to new and fascinating perspectives on some of history's most famous actors, Paul Kuttner has proven that the past can be illuminating and entertaining as well as tricky.

Joseph F. Kett
Professor of History
University of Virginia
Coauthor of *Dictionary of Cultural Literacy*

QUESTIONS

GENERAL HISTORY

☞ **Q 1.**

Name two Europeans who were born late in the nineteenth century at the same hour, in the same week, the same year. At times the two men also resembled each other physically and hated each other to the death. They probably changed the course of twentieth-century history in their respective worlds of politics and entertainment more than anyone else, and their faces are as familiar to people today as those of any human being, alive or dead. Who are these two men?

☞ **Q 2.**

Besides both having been Swedish diplomats, what did Raoul Wallenberg (1912–47), credited with saving thousands of Jews during World War II in Europe, and United Nations Secretary General Dag Hammarskjöld (1905–61) have in common?

QUESTIONS

☞ Q 3.

There is a forty-five-line typewritten letter dated October 11, 1939, at the FDR Library at Hyde Park, New York, urging President Roosevelt (1882–1945) to coordinate research on nuclear energy. Who instigated this letter to the president, and did it succeed in its stated aim?

☞ Q 4.

Why is the Civil War naval battle of the *Monitor* and the *Merrimack* misnamed?

☞ Q 5.

The French luxury liner, the *Normandie,* was either sabotaged or destroyed accidentally in New York Harbor during World War II. Nobody knows for sure what caused the fire that raged through the ship while it was being converted into a troopship in February 1942. Was that fire responsible for destroying the liner?

☞ Q 6.

Why was it impossible for the first Duke of Wellington to have made this observation: "The Battle of Waterloo was won on the playing fields of Eton"?

☞ Q 7.

What happened just outside Seymour, Indiana, on March 22, 1866—the consequences of which are still seen today throughout the United States? Hint: The crimes of Reno can even be felt in the state of Indiana.

GENERAL HISTORY

☞ **Q 8.**

A national convention was called to revise the Articles of Confederation in Philadelphia in 1787. During the great debate that ended with the signing of the Constitution on September 17, 1787, how much did Alexander Hamilton (1757–1804) and his New York delegation contribute to the fashioning of the Constitution?

☞ **Q 9.**

In this century a prime minister contacted the White House and the secretary of state to put pressure on an American to participate in a world championship. Who were the four participants in this odd transaction?

☞ **Q 10.**

For many years Aaron Burr (1756–1836) ignored the hostile remarks made about him by Alexander Hamilton. What exactly caused Burr to challenge Hamilton to a duel? And what was ironic about the location in Weehawken, New Jersey, where the duel was fought?

☞ **Q 11.**

Which king spoke poorly in his native tongue but well in the language of his hostile neighbor state?

☞ **Q 12.**

During the stormy days of the French Revolution, Robespierre became the head of the dreaded Committee of Public Safety on July 10, 1793, taking the place of the controversial Danton. This was the result of the insurrection of May 31, 1793. How did Danton feel about this setback engineered partly by his enemy Robespierre?

☞ Q 13.

During the French retreat from Moscow in 1812, the Russians defeated Napoleon. Was there ever a time before that date when Napoleon's gains were erased by a Russian?

☞ Q 14.

Were the thirty years following the Thirty Years' War (1618–48) known as the Thirty Years' Peace?

☞ Q 15.

Which European country failed to have its parliament in session for 175 years?

☞ Q 16.

Does the Non-Intercourse Act of 1809 have racial or moral implications? Specifically, whom was the act directed against?

☞ Q 17.

In the history of Europe, who had possibly the largest, best-organized empire? It stretched from Vienna to Baghdad, from Aden to Algiers, and from Cairo to the

Crimea. The ruler of this empire is still considered just, wise, and courteous, yet he had his eldest son strangled. He also signed a treaty with France against the Habsburgs in 1536, a friendship that lasted until late in the last century. Who was this man?

☞ **Q 18.**

Why didn't Robespierre ally himself with Danton during the French Revolution, at the height of Danton's power?

☞ **Q 19.**

Once the new American government was installed, in 1789, where was George Washington (1732–99) inaugurated, where did the first Supreme Court meet, and where was the Bill of Rights introduced?

☞ **Q 20.**

After declaring on August 8, 1945, that they would not occupy the northern half of Korea, how long did the Soviets wait before they went back on their word?

☞ **Q 21.**

What did Alexander Hamilton and Russia's greatest poet, Aleksandr Pushkin (1799–1837), have in common?

☞ **Q 22.**

When was the only posthumous award of the Nobel Peace Prize made?

QUESTIONS

☞ **Q 23.**

Who went to France late in the eighteenth century to market one of his many inventions: a pierless iron bridge? Hint: He was a British-American who made a name for himself in France.

☞ **Q 24.**

Was Hitler's Moscow defeat similar to Napoleon's in that the Russian winter brought untold chaos to both armies?

☞ **Q 25.**

Who instituted the practice of paying jurors a nominal fee for their services? Napoleon? Bismarck? Julius Caesar? Pericles? Ramses II? Queen Elizabeth I? Or was it mentioned somewhere in the Old Testament?

☞ **Q 26.**

Who made the following observations: That it was regrettable that the West had not resisted the Soviet Union in Eastern Europe while the United States in particular could still do so? That from then on, the best that could be expected of East-West relations was an armed truce? When asked what Stalin (1879–1953) would have done if the West had acceded to all his demands, the observer assured his questioner that Stalin would have come up immediately with another set of demands.

GENERAL HISTORY

☞ **Q 27.**

Which two prominent Americans wielding immense power in 1945 had this to say about dropping nuclear bombs on the Japanese cities of Hiroshima and Nagasaki?

1) "I had been conscious of a feeling of depression and so I voiced to him [Henry L. Stimson, secretary of war] my grave misgivings, first on the basis of my belief that Japan was already defeated and that dropping the bomb was completely unnecessary, and secondly because I thought that our country should avoid shocking world opinion by the use of a weapon whose employment was, I thought, no longer mandatory as a measure to save American lives."

2) "The Japanese were already defeated and ready to surrender. . . . The use of this barbarous weapon at Hiroshima and Nagasaki was of no material assistance in our war against Japan. . . . We adopted an ethical standard common to the barbarians of the Dark Ages."

☞ **Q 28.**

Beaten to their knees at the end of World War I and forced to sign an armistice in November 1918, Germany's troops had been defeated on all fronts and surrendered their arms to their enemies. True or false?

☞ **Q 29.**

As far back as 1834, the Kaffirs were constantly forced to trek to other regions, leaving their native Bantu lands in Africa because of the encroachment into their territory of the Dutch (Boer) cattlemen and farmers. How did the white Boers finally solve the black Kaffir problem when they could no longer use the natives as slaves after the abolition of slavery in South Africa in 1854?

☞ **Q 30.**

In 1516, Duke Wilhelm of Bavaria imposed the *Reinheitsgebot*—literally translated as the "purity command." Did this almost-five-hundred-year-old law stipulate racial purity similar to Hitler's Nuremberg Laws as far as the Bavarian population was concerned?

☞ **Q 31.**

What were the two greatest troop-carrying ships of all time, and what is the record number of troops carried during wartime?

☞ **Q 32.**

Who was the leading German Communist revolutionary immediately after the end of World War I, and what were this person's views on feminism and patriotism?

☞ **Q 33.**

Gaius Caesar started out as an extremely popular, benevolent Roman emperor. When he fell sick, his attitude changed drastically. Under which name was he best known to his subjects and to history, and what was the reason for it?

GENERAL HISTORY

☞ Q 34.

Which American wrote that the government had to be reconstituted, adding: "To be more contemptible than we already are is hardly possible"?

☞ Q 35.

Whatever became of Carolyne Long Banks, one of the young black organizers of the Atlanta student movement of the 1960s, who was arrested for demonstrating at Rich's, the huge Atlanta department store?

☞ Q 36.

What was hailed by writers such as Thoreau, Lowell, and even Whittier, the Quaker, as a great regenerative experience? A hint: Carl Sandburg and David O. Selznick would have agreed with these three men.

☞ Q 37.

In 1951, President Harry S Truman (1884–1972) fired General Douglas MacArthur (1880–1964) for his insubordination as commander of the U.N. forces in Korea. True or false?

☞ Q 38.

Which single event above everything else precipitated the fall of Saigon in 1975?

☞ Q 39.

In 1814, Napoleon (1769–1821) defeated the Prussians and Austria's Schwarzenberg five times in two weeks, then the Prussian Blücher four times the following week. Few generals in history had won so many battles in so short a time. Three weeks later, on March 27, Napoleon was victorious over Winzingerode at St. Dizier. What happened two weeks later?

☞ Q 40.

One of the black men who fought and got killed during the slave revolt at Harper's Ferry in 1859 was Lewis Sheridan Leary. A hundred years later, another African-American, Langston Hughes, made a name for himself as a poet. Apart from the fact that both men were fighters for the freedom of all men, what else did they share?

☞ Q 41.

When a plot was detected that implicated Mary Queen of Scots (1542–87) in the invasion of England by Spain, both houses of Parliament voted for her execution. Why did Queen Elizabeth I reject this step and keep Mary incarcerated at Sheffield Castle in 1572 only to reluctantly have her executed later?

☞ Q 42.

What reason did President William McKinley (1843–1901) give when he used U.S. troops to suppress the Philippine republic in 1898?

GENERAL HISTORY

☞ **Q 43.**

Which English king belonged to the brotherhood of troubadours and romancers, writing some of the finest lyrics of his time? Hint: Although a king for only a decade, he was always on the move, fighting, crusading, or being held prisoner, and virtually never setting foot in his own kingdom.

☞ **Q 44.**

What effect did President John F. Kennedy's 1962 speech have on the University of Mississippi's decision to allow James Meredith to enroll as the first African-American student?

☞ **Q 45.**

Who almost won World War I for the Germans, having caused the defeat of Russia, the Serbians, the Romanians, and Italy at Caporetto (1917), and nearly crushing the Allies in 1918 on the western front? Hint: Later, he fanatically endorsed the ideas of Hitler's crusades against the Jews, Catholics, Protestants, and Masons, then deserted Hitler and became a fierce pacifist.

☞ **Q 46.**

Which head of state ordered the assassination of an enemy military leader in one of this century's two world wars? Was the assassination attempt successful? If it failed, what were the consequences of the botched operation?

QUESTIONS

☞ **Q 47.**

Who was the first black woman allowed to become a social worker in the African Transkei?

☞ **Q 48.**

In the twentieth century two well-known grandsons went to war against each other. Who were the grandsons and who was their even more famous grandmother?

☞ **Q 49.**

Why was a knighted Irish leader executed by the British in 1916?

☞ **Q 50.**

When Captain James Cook first set foot in Australia in 1770, what were the first two recorded words with which he was welcomed by the aborigines?

☞ **Q 51.**

What were James Polk's four great objectives when he became president of the United States in 1845?

☞ **Q 52.**

How much damage did the Japanese midget submarines inflict on the United States in the Pacific theater during World War II?

☞ Q 53.

What was the almost immediate result of Washington's realization that the Articles of Confederation, drafted in 1777 and implemented in 1781, caused the states to begin bickering among themselves?

☞ Q 54.

Which nineteenth-century prince regent of a former colony declared its absolute independence from its European homeland against the demands of his father, then crowned himself as emperor of his adopted country?

☞ Q 55.

The English-speaking world was incensed by the Soviet Union's presence in Kabul, Afghanistan, when during the 1980s more than a hundred thousand Soviet troops occupied that country in order to bring it safely into the Soviet orbit. Years earlier, Russia and another world power had agreed that Russia's sphere of influence did not extend to Afghanistan. Russia did not abide by this agreement, and action was called for to rid Afghanistan of the Russians there. What did the Russians do in response?

☞ Q 56.

Why do so many British citizens cringe at the very mention of the fourth belly of the cow?

☞ Q 57.

Whose revolutionary teachings were banned in Russia at the end of the nineteenth century, and why were his followers banished to Siberia when it was discovered that his doctrine was published widely abroad?

☞ Q 58.

What percentage of U.S. prisoners of war died or were killed at the hands of their German Nazi captors? The Viet Cong? The Japanese in World War II? The North Koreans?

☞ Q 59.

What was the largest surrender of American forces in U.S. history?

☞ Q 60.

The Ukraine broke away from the Soviet Union in 1918, and the Ukrainian city of Odessa was ruled by the French and Belgians. True or false?

☞ Q 61.

Which queen of one country, after her first marriage was annulled, later married a man who became the king of another European country? And what were the consequences of these marriages over the next six hundred years?

☞ **Q 62.**

On December 9, 1986, thousands of students demonstrated for freedom and democracy in Heifei, the capital of Anhui Province in east-central China. Does December 9 have a special meaning for Chinese youths that scares Chinese authorities? What were the dire repercussions for some of China's future leaders of allowing the demonstration to happen?

☞ **Q 63.**

Which British philosopher had the greatest influence on Thomas Jefferson (1743–1826) and the Founding Fathers? And who, in turn, had influenced the thought of this British philosopher?

☞ **Q 64.**

On April 25, 1945, the United Nations Conference on International Organization convened in San Francisco, California, to draft the charter of the United Nations. Another historical event took place on the same day. What is the historical significance of that event?

☞ **Q 65.**

While the rest of the world denigrates Dracula as a bloodthirsty villain, why does Romania hail him as a hero?

☞ **Q 66.**

What feminist made this statement: "I never war against females, and it is only the base and cowardly that do"?

QUESTIONS

☞ Q 67.

Which European state (not country) modeled itself in the mid-nineteenth century after the British parliamentary system, because a leading statesman of that continental state was a liberal who was convinced of the importance of reform in all sectors of government?

☞ Q 68.

While the United States was busy fighting the revolutionary war against the British, the Continental Congress adopted the Articles of Confederation on November 15, 1777. Why did they not go into effect until March 1, 1781?

☞ Q 69.

What little-known French diplomat of the nineteenth century became world-famous in a field completely foreign to politics and diplomacy? Hint: The French government called him back to Paris in 1849 in disgrace, but this proved to be a blessing in disguise.

☞ Q 70.

King George III was not the monster depicted in so many American novels. He was well-read and a virtuous monarch, always battling with arrogant politicians to maintain a proper constitutional place in the British system of government. What was his one weakness, which helped to put an end to his dream of solidifying and enlarging the empire?

☞ **Q 71.**

After the French withdrew from Vietnam in 1954, were all of their captured soldiers returned immediately as promised by the Communist Vietnamese?

☞ **Q 72.**

Who was the youngest U.S. president in the nineteenth century?

☞ **Q 73.**

Who was the first African-American teenager in the United States to become a celebrated case for her civil rights crusade?

☞ **Q 74.**

Where did the bearded figure and name of Uncle Sam originate?

☞ **Q 75.**

In what affectionate terms did the first lieutenant governor of Australia describe the island continent?

☞ **Q 76.**

Historians call it one of the decisive battles of history. It took place in the eighth decade of the eighteenth century. One of the forces, a ragged army, was led by a timid leader, but one of his generals was finally responsible for staging a victory. The brave general, though wounded in action, led his army to a great and decisive victory. Who were the participants, and what were the consequences of the battles?

☞ **Q 77.**

Did the Founding Fathers phrase the U.S. Constitution in such a way that it would help to abolish slavery? How much would it have helped the slaves if the signers had worded the Constitution differently?

☞ **Q 78.**

What are the facts and ironies concerning the cases of two famous ships? The name of the first ship starts with the letter *t*. The ship left port in April and ran up an iceberg starboard near midnight. It was going twenty-five knots at the time. It was capable of carrying 3,000 people and sank, even though it was considered unsinkable because of its sixteen watertight compartments. The name of the second ship starts with the letter *m*. The captain of this liner was E. J. Smith. What do the two ships have in common?

☞ **Q 79.**

In the 1930s and early 1940s, the Japanese army occupying China followed the orders of the Tokyo-directed anti-Communist "pacification" program of *sanko-seisaku:* "Kill all, burn all, destroy all." They invaded the regions dominated by the Chinese Communists, led by Mao, and reduced the population there from 44 million to what by the end of World War II?

☞ Q 80.

This wife of a head of state spent as much as $1.35 million a year on her clothing. Another year she spent $2.7 million on a single pair of diamond earrings. Her personal debts came to $2 million. When she was thrown out by the people it never occurred to her why she was held in such contempt. Even her mother was embarrassed by her daughter's wasteful behavior. Who was this woman?

☞ Q 81.

Who was the first American politician to endorse the product of a soap manufacturer?

☞ Q 82.

Who were the first storm troopers?

☞ Q 83.

Who made the following statement: "Why have such a beautiful action marred by any taint of legality"?

☞ Q 84.

He was the son of a vinegar manufacturer, and during World War II he became a POW of the Germans. Three times he made his escape from them; the third time he was lucky enough not to be recaptured. After the war he entered politics and later became a head of state. Who is he?

☞ Q 85.

Provoked by antiwar agitation, President Abraham Lincoln (1809–65) was compelled to undertake steps that could be considered antidemocratic. True or false?

☞ Q 86.

Of the 103 passengers who sailed on the *Mayflower* from Plymouth, England, on September 6, 1620 (Old Style), how many survived the trip and landed near what is now Plymouth, Massachusetts? What reason did the vessel's crew give for the Pilgrim Fathers' decision to land there on December 11, 1620 (Old Style), December 21, 1620 (New Style)?

☞ Q 87.

Who made the following statement: "A little rebellion now and then is a good thing, and as necessary in the political world as storms in the physical.... It is a medicine necessary for the sound health of government"?

☞ Q 88.

The United States sent weapons to the anti-Communist contras in the 1980s to fight the left-wing government authorities in Nicaragua. Where were most of these weapons manufactured?

☞ **Q 89.**

Union officer Captain George Todd was responsible for quite a victory in November 1863, yet history books fail to mention his exploits. Why?

☞ **Q 90.**

What is unique about Pakistan's Prime Minister Benazir Bhutto (b. 1953) among all twentieth-century heads of government?

☞ **Q 91.**

What famous battle in the twentieth century was fought by the French not for military gains but more for idealistic reasons?

☞ **Q 92.**

In addition to Stalin's slaughter of countless Georgians in 1922, what else caused Lenin to break away from Stalin?

☞ **Q 93.**

What is one of the most famous instances in the history of India in which Hindus and Muslims lived, worked, and profited side by side, although not peacefully, and in doing so added a word to the English language?

☞ **Q 94.**

Which European king invited which foreign philosopher to his palace for a short time in the eighteenth century and had a stormy, rather than cordial, relationship with him?

☞ **Q 95.**

Why did the workers of Russia turn against Kerenski (1881–1970) and the February 1917 revolution but embrace Lenin (1870–1924) and his October 1917 revolution?

☞ **Q 96.**

Which one of Hitler's generals was brave enough to warn the Nazi dictator about the oncoming winter campaign as Hitler was approaching Moscow? Did the following conversation really take place or was it taken from a well-known novel? If the latter, from which novel was it extracted?

"The winter is the big difficulty to begin with. The lack of stores, of horses for your artillery, of transfer for your sick and wounded, stout fur-lined gloves, a cap with eartabs, warm boot-socks, heavy boots to keep his feet from getting frostbitten. You lack all this. . . ."

But the head of state would not be budged. "The extreme rigors of winter do not come on in twenty-four hours," he said. "Although we are less acclimatized than the Russians, we are fundamentally more robust.

We have not had autumn yet. We shall have plenty of time before winter sets in." And the general replied, "Winter will come like a bombshell—and you cannot be too apprehensive, considering the present state of the army."

☞ **Q 97.**

Why did Czar Nicholas II himself take supreme command of the Russian armies on September 5, 1915, and what was the purpose of his first offensive, the Battle of Lake Naroch?

☞ **Q 98.**

Why was Cesare Borgia's recapture, in 1502, of the dukedom of Urbino by the Papal States referred to as one of history's most despicable treacheries?

☞ **Q 99.**

When the Russian Brusilov offensive of June 1916 coincided with Joffre's great offensive on the Somme, as planned by the French and the Russians, did the Russian victories at Czernowitz and Lutsk help their morale and contribute to a more definite Russian victory in 1916?

☞ **Q 100.**

He was a hero in America's War of Independence. Later he became a commander of the constitutional and initially responsible citizen-militia in France, was declared a traitor and jailed in Austria for allegedly being an active revolutionary. Who was this man? Hint: Napoleon considered him a "simpleton," and the U.S. Congress voted a gift of $200,000 and a township of land in his honor.

☞ Q 101.

This woman was married to Prince George of Greece, yet she had many amorous affairs. She was a patient of Sigmund Freud and later risked her life rescuing Jews from the Nazis. She was also the person who established psychoanalysis in France. Who was she? Hint: She bore one of the most famous names in history, the name of a man who traveled widely in Europe and Egypt.

☞ Q 102.

Books and articles have claimed that Thomas Jefferson took a black slave from his estate for a mistress, without exempting her from any of her menial duties. How much of this is true, how much legend?

☞ Q 103.

Why did President Ronald Reagan (b. 1911) accelerate the buildup of the Rapid Deployment Force (RDF) early in his administration?

☞ Q 104.

In which eighteenth-century war did two allies, after a succession of victories, suffer such a heavy defeat that both would have lost the war if the enemy had not with-drawn its forces, enabling the two allies to be final vic-tors after all?

☞ **Q 105.**

Who assumed the mantle of rebel leadership against his will, did not want to resort to arms, was helpless to stem the tide of events, was granted a pardon for his earlier and unblemished participation in the American Revolution, and finally died poor and unlamented by his onetime comrades-in-arms?

☞ **Q 106.**

In many paintings Stalin can be seen greeting Lenin as he descends from the train in Belo-Ostrov and Petrograd, returning in April 1917 from his long exile. All official accounts pay tribute to this welcoming scene as well. Are these reports and paintings based on fact?

☞ **Q 107.**

Why did the start of the American Civil War in 1861 have a disastrous effect on Britain?

☞ **Q 108.**

Is there any proof that the Catholic Mary Queen of Scots could be blamed, directly or indirectly, for the burning at the stake of hundreds of English Protestants in the sixteenth century?

QUESTIONS

☞ **Q 109.**

Who was the last prisoner to be jailed in the Tower of London?

☞ **Q 110.**

First came the Constitution in 1787. Then the ten amendments known as the Bill of Rights were incorporated into the Constitution. How is it possible that the Bill of Rights actually influenced the Constitution of the United States?

☞ **Q 111.**

What is the largest number of armies that faced each other simultaneously on various battlefields in the same war?

☞ **Q 112.**

When Julius Caesar, Claudius, and Hadrian invaded England in the first centuries before and after Christ, they intended to invade Scotland as well, but they changed their minds. True or false? Also, is it true or false that their influence on English life was passed on to future generations and reaches into our era?

☞ **Q 113.**

What ever happened to Aelia Capitolina? And what would most likely have happened if Emperor Hadrian had not died in A.D. 138?

☞ **Q 114.**

What was the primary reason Mohandas Karamchand Gandhi (1869–1948) left South Africa for India in July 1914?

☞ **Q 115.**

What single event fired British Prime Minister Lloyd George's mind not only to fight for a Jewish homeland in Palestine, but to become a fast friend of Chaim Weizmann?

☞ **Q 116.**

When American soldiers entered Paris in the summer of 1944, they were seen strolling down the Champs Elysées with two or more French girls on their arms. What famous American journalist made a very witty statement in response to this?

☞ **Q 117.**

Although Jews were expelled from Vienna in 1670, Maria Theresa, queen of Hungary and Bohemia and archduchess of Austria, did not order them out of Bohemia until 1747. What happened after she made her edict?

☞ **Q 118.**

American Indians saw their livelihood threatened by the white settlers in Illinois in the late 1820s, and out of this conflict a war began in 1832. The resultant peace treaties of 1832 and 1833 finally broke Indian power within the state. There was one U.S. company captain who briefly fought in that war and who later became famous in the United States and abroad. Who was this captain and what was the war he fought in known as?

☞ **Q 119.**

Which country was the last to declare war on Germany in World War I?

☞ **Q 120.**

Until around the mid-1850s, only members of the Church of England could enter the universities of Oxford and Cambridge and sit in Parliament in England. True or false?

☞ **Q 121.**

Was the assassination of the Austro-Hungarian heir apparent to the throne, Archduke Francis Ferdinand, at Sarajevo, the capital of Bosnia and Herzegovina, on June 28, 1914, the primary reason World War I broke out?

☞ **Q 122.**

Is the best-established record of an invasion also the first battle known in detail in history? When and where did it take place?

GENERAL HISTORY

☞ **Q 123.**

Is it true or false that the Danes were bribed in the post-war period by the English with Danish money (*Danegeld*) to further the economic aims of the English people?

☞ **Q 124.**

For about half a century after 1810, a little-remembered British statesman dominated the course of the British Empire. He served as secretary of war, foreign secretary, and prime minister. He became one of the most forceful statesmen and liberal-minded Tories, and later became a Whig. Who was he? And what was his attitude toward the American Civil War?

☞ **Q 125.**

Two years after the *Titanic* sank in 1912, another equally horrible maritime disaster occurred. What was it?

☞ **Q 126.**

Who was memorialized by the first mourning stamps on record to be issued *outside* the country of birth of the deceased?

☞ **Q 127.**

Who had an honorable burial in London's Westminster Abbey, yet whose corpse was disinterred three years later and hung on the gallows?

QUESTIONS

☞ **Q 128.**

Why didn't the British government after World War I try to make economic accommodations with the Arabs in order to win their favor in light of the increasing Jewish population in Palestine? That population rose from one Jew in fifteen in 1919 (about 6.5 percent of the population) to one Jewish immigrant for every three Palestinian inhabitants (about 33 percent) in 1939.

☞ **Q 129.**

What single action can be credited to Napoleon's charismatic appeal to his men and was perhaps the most important reason for his successes after 1796?

☞ **Q 130.**

Why did the great Greek historian Thucydides (460–400 B.C.) consider the war of 431–421 B.C. (the Archidamian War) and the war of 414–404 B.C. (the Ionian War) to be one war, although they were fought at different times in different territories?

☞ **Q 131.**

Where did the American Congress first settle before the Confederation came to an end in 1790?

☞ **Q 132.**

Who served as a delegate to the Continental Congress for two states from the 1760s to the 1780s? A hint:

GENERAL HISTORY

These states were among the first to ratify the Constitution.

☞ **Q 133.**

In one of the wars between the British East-India Company and Indian troops, the British Governor General Wellesley was ordered to defeat Tippoo Sahib, who, in 1799, was corresponding with Napoleon in hopes that Napoleon would rescue him and the Indian state of Mysore. However, the governor general's brother, Arthur, won the last of the Mysore wars, killing Tippoo Sahib. Later, history knew the brother by what other name?

☞ **Q 134.**

George Washington became the first president of the United States on April 30, 1789. Who said at the time that he was "afraid that the republic would not last beyond his lifetime"?

☞ **Q 135.**

Initially, who was the most powerful and pivotal figure supporting the Balfour Declaration, which was made on November 2, 1917, and designed to establish a Jewish homeland in Palestine?

☞ **Q 136.**

Which British-American writer refuted Edmund Burke's hostile thesis about the French Revolution, and what were the consequences of his writings?

QUESTIONS

☞ **Q 137.**

Married presidential candidate Gary Hart (b. 1937) temporarily withdrew from the presidential race when it was learned that he had spent a night with a young actress, Donna Rice, in 1987. And another Democratic presidential candidate, Arkansas Governor Bill Clinton (b. 1946), was in deep trouble with the media when sometime-cabaret singer Gennifer Flowers claimed in 1992 that she and Clinton had had a twelve-year affair. There was a more famous figure in American history who had been lured into an affair with a married woman while he himself was married. This liaison was leaked to the press, which made the most of it. Who was this politician? And how did the political outcome differ from the result of Senator Hart's indiscretions?

☞ **Q 138.**

What do these three unrelated items have in common? It is the first full day in court for Nazi war criminal Adolf Eichmann (1906–62), who went on trial in Jerusalem the previous day. President John F. Kennedy (1917–63) announces at a news conference that there will be no U.S. intervention in Cuba five days before the Bay of Pigs invasion by Cuban exiles. Soviet cosmonaut Yuri Gagarin (1934–68) is the first man to fly in outer space.

☞ **Q 139.**

The people who contributed the word *commando* to the English language were victims in the first concentration camps in this century. Who were the prisoners? And who was responsible for establishing this sort of cruel treatment in camps built especially for these prisoners?

☞ Q 140.

Did the South Africa Act of 1909, culminating in the Union of South Africa in 1910, become law when voted on in the administrative government building in Cape Town, and did it bar blacks from sitting in this governmental body?

☞ Q 141.

Did somebody actually call Richard M. Nixon soft on Communism? If so, who was the person?

☞ Q 142.

What code did the samurai of feudal Japan live by?

☞ Q 143.

Did George Washington ever smoke marijuana?

☞ Q 144.

In more than sixty years of this century, no democratically elected president has been able to serve out his full term peacefully in which country?

QUESTIONS

☞ **Q 145.**

A nasty Roman emperor had a sister who was accused of poisoning her second husband and then married her uncle and persuaded him to make her son by a previous marriage heir to the throne in place of his own son. Finally she poisoned her uncle. Who was she, and how did her son express his gratitude to her?

☞ **Q 146.**

After Napoleon had captured Alexandria and Cairo in July 1798, who cut off his victorious armies from his French homeland, and what were the consequences of this battle?

☞ **Q 147.**

Which one of the original thirteen states of the United States of America refused to send a delegation to the 1787 Constitutional Convention in Philadelphia, and why?

☞ **Q 148.**

When was the entire male population of one country conscripted and pressed into active military service?

☞ **Q 149.**

Nazis always had Gestapo officers watching the goings-on in World War II German army headquarters. Similarly, Soviet commissars attended Soviet military headquarters under Stalin. Were commissars also spy-

ing on European generals in the eighteenth century? If
they were, on what occasion?

☞ **Q 150.**

In which country did the native language gradually dis-
appear as a form of oral communication but survive in
written usage?

☞ **Q 151.**

Shortly after the end of the Korean War, the United
States began to integrate African-Americans into the
Reserve and National Guard. When did Massachusetts
change its laws to allow African-Americans to serve in
the organized militia?

☞ **Q 152.**

Who was the last Habsburg emperor and where is he
buried?

☞ **Q 153.**

What is the great irony about the Curtiss JN4-H
biplane bearing the serial number 38262, which took
off from Washington's Potomac Park for Philadelphia
on May 15, 1918?

☞ **Q 154.**

Which American first lady was accused of being a spy,
then had her son bring insanity proceedings against

her, and was finally committed to a sanatorium before he became secretary of war?

☞ Q 155.

Which military dictator, dead for a century and a half, is venerated and has monuments in his honor in fourteen countries?

☞ Q 156.

The French government honored the 369th U.S. Infantry for its valor in World War I with the Croix de Guerre, France's highest military honor. What was so special about this infantry regiment?

☞ Q 157.

Whom or what did George Washington refer to as "a child of fortune, to be fostered by some and buffeted by others"?

☞ Q 158.

What is unique about the fact that Michael (Mihai) of Romania ruled from 1927 to 1930, and Carol II of Romania ascended the throne in 1930 and reigned until 1940?

☞ Q 159.

What happened two hundred years ago in French history to remind us of the Iran-contra affair, in which monies were solicited from third parties to support a foreign venture?

☞ Q 160.

On June 25, 1941, President Franklin D. Roosevelt signed a law that went largely unnoticed in most newspapers at the time but had tremendous ramifications. What law became effective on that date?

☞ Q 161.

In November 1775 General George Washington signed an order that he rescinded a month later. What did the original order proclaim?

☞ Q 162.

In the United States, President John F. Kennedy shared something with author Aldous Huxley. So did singer Edith Piaf with playwright Jean Cocteau in France, and Stalin with composer Prokofiev in the Soviet Union. What exactly did they share?

☞ Q 163.

Who wrote the American Constitution?

☞ Q 164.

Was the main reason that the Soviet Union celebrated its October Revolution in November attributable to the fact that the Winter Palace in Petrograd (later Leningrad, now St. Petersburg) was stormed in November 1917?

☞ Q 165.

Was the 1912 *Titanic* disaster or the 1987 *Victor–Dona Paz* collision, some 110 miles south of Manila, the Philippines, the worst calamity at sea of all time?

☞ Q 166.

Which American first lady was baptized with these names: Claudia Alta?

☞ Q 167.

What are the three photos most frequently ordered by the public from the photo section of the National Archives of the United States?

☞ Q 168.

Name at least six perplexing coincidences concerning the U.S. presidents Abraham Lincoln and John F. Kennedy.

☞ Q 169.

Why was St. Eustatius, a small island in the West Indies, one of the focal points of world history two centuries ago?

GENERAL HISTORY

☞ **Q 170.**

One of the earliest groups of Jewish immigrants to the Dutch colonial city of New Amsterdam were newcomers fleeing the Inquisition in Brazil in 1654. How did they celebrate their religious freedom on arriving in the New World?

☞ **Q 171.**

What happened to the thousands of books Thomas Jefferson had in his Virginia mansion, Monticello?

☞ **Q 172.**

From a historical point of view, what was unique about Asser Levy?

☞ **Q 173.**

The father worked as a butler for the man who governed his country, yet the son later became a Duke. Who was the son?

☞ **Q 174.**

He was one of the mightiest rulers, yet about half a century after he drowned, his historical achievements virtually crumbled. Who was this ruler, and why did many of his immediate Christian followers commit suicide or become Muslims after his death?

QUESTIONS

☞ Q 175.

Which emperor taught himself to write as an adult, helped to design one of the great cathedrals of the world, and is claimed as a national hero by two countries?

☞ Q 176.

Even before he was thirty years old, in the 1920s, he had won the European lightweight boxing championship and had become a millionaire manufacturing can openers, radios, automobiles, phonographs, and airplanes. Yet he became much more famous in the 1970s and 1980s for his World War II exploits. Who was this man, and what did he do that made him so famous?

☞ Q 177.

Who was commissioned in the last century to compose the melody to the American national anthem "The Star-Spangled Banner"? Or did its lyricist, Francis Scott Key (1779–1843), compose the music himself?

☞ Q 178.

During the French Revolution the guillotine sliced off the heads of priests and paupers, royalty and revolutionaries, even claiming the lives of Danton (1759–94) and Robespierre (1758–94). How soon after the Revolution was death by guillotine abolished in France?

☞ Q 179.

Who first made the comment, "Let them eat cake!" in the eighteenth century?

☞ Q 180.

What did President George Bush (b. 1924) find so intriguing about Franklin D. Roosevelt's middle name that he felt he could relate to it?

☞ Q 181.

Who said: "That's one small step for man, one giant leap for mankind"?

☞ Q 182.

Why would the consequences of a queen's outliving each of her seventeen children prove to be embarrassing to a German composer? Who were the queen and the composer?

☞ Q 183.

Who was the first black politician in the United States to serve as the governor of a state?

☞ Q 184.

Approximately when did the following statement appear on the editorial page of the *New York Times:* "One week ago Russia came of age. She allowed her people all the fun and trappings of a real election—voting not publicly by a show of hands but in private in red-curtained booths behind closed doors"?

☞ **Q 185.**

In the twentieth century Allied naval forces bombarded the coastal installations of a peninsula to capture an enemy capital about 130 miles away. Why is it no longer the capital and what is the new name of that city?

When the naval operation did not succeed, the Allies landed on the peninsula to achieve their objectives. Did they succeed this time?

In classical geography the place is known as the Thracian Chersonese. Its countrymen today call it Gelibolu in the province of Çanakkale. By what name is this locale and the military campaign known in the Western world?

☞ **Q 186.**

What minor German-born princess (of Anhalt-Zerbst) was betrothed at fifteen, then overthrew her powerful husband eighteen years later and established herself as the head of the largest territorial and political area in modern history?

☞ **Q 187.**

Which royalty wrote an autobiography conversing with God, a synopsis of his or her reign, and a collection of maxims? This royal person was also a linguist, a student of philosophy, unmistakably homosexual, a lover of absolute power, and even lured René Descartes (1596–

1650) to an early death. Then the monarch converted from Protestantism to Catholicism, abdicated, and schemed to become monarch of another country, later falling in love with Cardinal Azzolino, and finally dying as a result of a fit of regal bad temper. This individual is the only royal personage to be buried in the crypt in Saint Peter's.

☞ Q 188.

Who made the following two predictions in September 1919? "I can predict with absolute certainty that within another generation there will be another world war, if the nations of the world do not concert the method by which to prevent it." And: "What the Germans used were toys compared to what would be used in the next war." What happened to the speaker almost immediately after he made these observations?

☞ Q 189.

Was Catherine the Great of Russia ever secretly married?

☞ Q 190.

What was the common experience in the romantic lives of Queen Elizabeth I and Queen Christina of Sweden?

☞ Q 191.

Who was the rather colorless, long-forgotten character whose one famous utterance is: "What this country needs is a good five-cent cigar"? Hint: The bitter irony is that if another man had died, this man would have changed the history of the twentieth century for the better.

☞ Q 192.

What is the world's oldest independent republic, and was this state among the first ten, the first twenty, or the first thirty nations to become a full member of the United Nations?

☞ Q 193.

When Menachem Begin (1913–92) was the head of the Zionist underground organization Irgun Zvai Leumi in the 1940s, from whom did he obtain most of the weapons and explosives to liberate Palestine from British colonial rule? How did Begin spend his time in Palestine just prior to the liberation struggle in 1943?

☞ Q 194.

Can you name the people who made these predictions?

A) "The South has too much common sense and good temper to break up the Union." (1860)

B) "That's an amazing invention, but who would ever want to use one of them?" (1876, after witnessing a demonstration of the telephone)

C) "The phonograph is of no commercial value." (1880)

D) "Believe me, Germany is unable to wage war." (1934)

E) "No matter what happens, the United States Navy is

not going to be caught napping." (December 4, 1941)

F) "The United States will not be a threat to us [Germany] for decades—not in 1945, but at the earliest 1970 or 1980."

☞ Q 195.

Which British prime minister was so sick that he could not deliver his resignation to Queen Elizabeth II at her private residence, the Sandringham House in Norfolk?

☞ Q 196.

In the most unexpected upheaval of his political career, Winston Churchill (1874–1965) lost his Conservative premiership to Labour's Clement Attlee (1883–1967) during the Potsdam Conference in July 1945, just after he had led his country successfully through World War II. What was so ironic about this election defeat, in light of the general election almost forty years earlier in Great Britain?

☞ Q 197.

Can you name one of the most celebrated Americans in the last century and a half to change party affiliations only four years before becoming president?

WORLD WAR II AND THE NAZIS

☞ **Q 1.**

The Ultra Turing decoder gave the British government the ability to eavesdrop on every final decision the Nazi High Command made about a forthcoming battle or military campaign during World War II, by decoding the messages sent out over the Germans' Enigma machine. However, what went wrong for the Allies in the Battle of the Bulge, shortly before the end of the war in the European theater, leaving them completely unprepared for Hitler's (1889–1945) final offensive?

☞ **Q 2.**

In each of the following two incidents of World War II, a rumor has crept in. Over the decades since these two events occurred these rumors have been accepted as fact. Can you tell which legend varies slightly from what really happened?

WORLD WAR II AND THE NAZIS

1) When the Germans who tried to assassinate Hitler on July 20, 1944, with the intent of starting a new government and bringing the war to an end, were captured by the Nazis, they were sentenced to death and hung on meat hooks with piano wire. The filmed account of these executions was destroyed on Hitler's orders after he had watched it three times in his private movie theater.

2) After the British cracked the Nazi code network through the 1938 sale by a Pole, "Lewinski," of the Enigma code machine, Winston Churchill (1874–1965) learned a few days prior to the Nazi attack on Coventry that the Germans were to bomb the English city. However, he could not deploy the full strength of the RAF's defensive forces against the Luftwaffe since it might have tipped off the Berlin government that the British knew of the aerial attack beforehand. Then the Nazis would have changed their code and the wiring of their Enigma rotors to make it impossible for London to crack it. Therefore, Coventry had to be sacrificed.

☞ Q 3.

Here are two events that allegedly happened during World War II. One of these statements, however, does not quite tally with the facts. Can you tell which observation in these statements is untrue and never really happened?

1) There was a military operation known by the code name "Canned Goods." If this is true, when and where did it take place?

2) When the Nazis occupied Denmark, they ordered all Jews to wear the Star of David so it was visible when they were out in public. The king of Denmark, Christian X, and hundreds of thousands of Danes also pinned the

Star of David on their clothes as a gesture of defiance and solidarity with their Jewish co-citizens and to confuse the German occupation troops. It succeeded in saving almost half the Danish Jews, who were smuggled to Sweden during the war.

☞ **Q 4.**

Nazi Germany's most celebrated U-boat commander, Günther Prien, penetrated Scapa Flow in the Orkney Islands (off the northeastern tip of Scotland) and sank the British battleship HMS *Royal Oak* soon after World War II began. In July 1940, he sank the British passenger ship the *Arondora Star*. Why was this a greater loss to Germany than to Great Britain?

☞ **Q 5.**

He married Richard Wagner's daughter, Eva, and wrote a book in 1899, *Die Grundlagen des 19. Jahrhunderts* (*The Foundations of the Nineteenth Century*). This book created the Aryan, pan-German myth by blaming the Jews for debasing what allegedly was best in the German character. It influenced Hitler more than any other work. Who was this man?

☞ **Q 6.**

What happened to the bulk of the gold (including gold teeth extracted from concentration camp prisoners), platinum, diamonds, and foreign currency taken from Europe's Nazi victims in World War II?

WORLD WAR II AND THE NAZIS

☞ **Q 7.**

Who was the first person to realize that one day the Nazi Holocaust might be presented to the world as nothing but propaganda? When did this person fear that such lies might be spread about the decimation of the Jews?

☞ **Q 8.**

In the 1940s, there was a mysterious program called Operation Paperclip. What was it, and why did it have this name?

☞ **Q 9.**

Hitler did not direct the Holocaust only against the Jewish people but against the gypsies of Europe as well. He succeeded in wiping out between 500,000 and 1,000,000 of them on the Continent, except for the most famous gypsy. Who was this gypsy, and why did the Nazis overlook him? What terrible accident, which threatened his life and career, did he have to overcome?

☞ **Q 10.**

Was the decision to scuttle the German battleship *Admiral Graf Spee* on December 17, 1939, in the territorial waters of Uruguay based on Captain Langsdorff's fear of engaging in a sea battle with the two British light cruisers *Ajax* and *Achilles* and the heavy cruiser *Cumberland*? If not, what other reason was there for its scuttling? And how did Hitler feel about it?

QUESTIONS

☞ **Q 11.**

During World War II, 1942 and 1943 were catastrophic years for the Allied merchant marine and their convoys. On the average, five Allied vessels were sunk daily. The German U-boat "wolf pack" tactic was eminently successful and almost brought Great Britain to her knees. Why were these Nazi "wolf packs" so successful in sinking so many of the Allied convoys? Why couldn't the Allies decode Nazi messages of the whereabouts of the U-boats when Great Britain had the capacity to do so with its Ultra Turing engine since the beginning of the war?

☞ **Q 12.**

Hitler's intelligence chief, Admiral Wilhelm Canaris (1887–1945), was always surprised that the information he leaked to the Allies through his *Schwarze Kapelle* secret group was mostly ignored by the British. Did the British not trust Canaris?

☞ **Q 13.**

She was the sister of a world-famous nineteenth-century writer who was bedridden for the last eleven years of his life, suffering from a syphilis-related deterioration of the brain. While he was dying, the sister wrested all his literary rights from their aging mother. But afterward she became a well-known writer in her own right and was nominated three times for the Nobel Prize in literature. She befriended Hitler, who not only donated money to her brother's archives but presided over her funeral in 1935. Who was this German woman?

☞ **Q 14.**

What German with a famous last name helped to hide Jews and save them from deportation to Nazi death camps in World War II?

☞ **Q 15.**

How did the chief of Hitler's intelligence apparatus (*Abwehr*) during World War II, Admiral Canaris, get rid of some Jews in a particularly audacious manner?

☞ **Q 16.**

In Nazi Germany, about 90 to 95 percent of the German Jews (around a half million were still living there at the outset of World War II) were exterminated by the Nazis during the war. What percentage of Jews from Fascist Italy were killed during the Holocaust?

☞ **Q 17.**

On what occasion did Hitler shake the hand of a Jew, feeling very pleased with himself, as he admitted later?

☞ **Q 18.**

Was the Führer's drive to become the head of a Pan-European world power solely provoked by Germany's failure to be the victor of World War I and its subsequent economic deterioration?

QUESTIONS

☞ **Q 19.**

Could the American advance through Europe in 1944 be credited mostly to the aggressiveness of U.S. ground troops or to the mechanical operations of war?

☞ **Q 20.**

Which person, who later became a missionary, was present at the following three events: the attack on Pearl Harbor on December 7, 1941; the bombing of Hiroshima on August 6, 1945; the surrender ceremonies on board the battleship USS *Missouri* on September 2, 1945, in Tokyo Bay?

☞ **Q 21.**

Under the Mussolini (1883–1945) dictatorship, Jews were deprived of their ability to raise money for Jewish charities; Jewish patients were not entitled to receive kosher food in hospitals or have access to their own religious services there or in Jewish old-age homes; and no Jew in any Italian enterprise was permitted to take days off on Jewish holidays. How soon after Mussolini's fall (1945) were these anti-Semitic laws rescinded?

☞ **Q 22.**

In the weeks leading up to the French Armistice on June 22, 1940, approximately how many troops, including those from Dunkirk, were evacuated from France and

landed safely in Great Britain? How many of these were
evacuated from Dunkirk?

☞ Q 23.

Did Mengele ever meet Hitler?

☞ Q 24.

Has it been established when the first large-scale military air transport in history took place?

☞ Q 25.

Hitler is believed to have apologized in public only once after coming to power in 1933. On what occasion and to whom did he apologize?

☞ Q 26.

Shortly before Hitler committed suicide in his Berlin bunker on April 30, 1945, he appointed the commander in chief of the German navy, Admiral Karl Dönitz, to be Nazi Germany's new Führer. Was Admiral Dönitz the last head of the Nazi navy?

☞ Q 27.

Did Stalin, himself an anti-Semite, order the execution of thousands of Soviet anti-Semites for other than ideological or economic reasons?

QUESTIONS

☞ **Q 28.**

Did Mussolini's performance in his seven-month war (1935–36) against the virtually defenseless Abyssinians influence Hitler in making the Duce the less powerful partner of the Berlin-Rome Axis?

☞ **Q 29.**

What is the only country in Europe that was conquered, occupied, and ruled by the Soviets, but in which Western-style democracy has survived to this day?

☞ **Q 30.**

The lull in fighting after Hitler conquered Poland in September 1939, which lasted until his invasion of France, Belgium, the Netherlands, Denmark, and Norway in the spring of 1940, was known as the Phony War. What was Hitler's principal reason for postponing his planned invasion of the Low Countries from October 1939 until the spring of 1940?

☞ **Q 31.**

Nazi Foreign Minister von Ribbentrop had his own representative at the January 1942 Wannsee Conference, where it was decided that the "Final Solution of the Jewish Question" would be to exterminate every single Jew in Europe. What was the representative's name? Ironically, he had the same name as the best-known anti-Semite of the sixteenth century.

☞ **Q 32.**

Which one of the following items must be wrong?

1) There was an out-and-out Nazi whose mission was to destroy the Allies in World War II. He succeeded eminently and later did everything in his power to help the very countries he tried to destroy—Great Britain and the United States—to build up the postwar German air force.

2) Hitler did not object when someone who was not a member of his inner circle fastened on his belt and pistol before going to have a private lunch with the Nazi dictator.

3) A few weeks after D day, Hitler admitted to a low-ranking officer of the Luftwaffe that the war was lost for Germany. He then listened to this officer criticize some of the Führer's policies—after which Hitler actually went out of his way to praise the officer.

☞ **Q 33.**

There was a successful seizure of all government buildings by a monarchist group in Berlin after World War I—a group that supported the workers of Germany. Yet the coup failed. Why? When did this coup take place and under what name is it known? Why did this and another coup, conducted at the same time, have a lasting effect on Germany's future?

☞ **Q 34.**

In a twentieth-century battle, control of an area of land changed every twelve hours for days, with one navy and air force supplying manpower to the area during the daylight hours, while the enemy did exactly the same thing during the night. What battle was this, and when did it take place?

☞ Q 35.

The very last handwritten order Hitler gave in his bunker on April 24, 1945, was addressed to General Steiner, demanding immediate military relief in Berlin. Who actually received this message?

☞ Q 36.

In 1942, Hitler almost succeeded in starving Britain into submission. What were the two primary factors that prevented this disaster?

☞ Q 37.

With the RAF's swift Spitfires and Hurricanes being pressed into service almost immediately after Britain entered World War II on September 3, 1939, the slow-moving German dirigible *Graf Zeppelin* could hardly be called upon to serve the Nazi war effort. A month before the war broke out, however, it did help to prepare Germany for fighting in World War II. Exactly what mission did the slow airship perform and was it successful?

☞ Q 38.

Rumors persist that President Franklin D. Roosevelt knew about the impending attack by the Japanese on

WORLD WAR II AND THE NAZIS

Pearl Harbor and that he let it happen in order to enter the war on the side of the Allies. Did he really know before December 1941 that the Japanese were planning to stage a surprise attack on Pearl Harbor?

☞ **Q 39.**

Why was an outmoded U.S. destroyer—the *Buchanan*—which was built in 1919, so important to the Allies in 1942, after her funnels had been cut off?

☞ **Q 40.**

Who wrote Nazi Germany's National Socialist anthem before he was killed by the Communists?

☞ **Q 41.**

Few places in London were as safe from Nazi bombs during World War II as the subway, or underground, stations. Did bombs ever cause injuries to people there?

☞ **Q 42.**

Exactly when was the Nazi salute imposed throughout the German armed forces?

☞ **Q 43.**

Himmler's SS liaison with Hitler was General Karl Wolff, who was also helpful to the Allies after the war in negotiating to have the German forces lay down their arms in Italy. How did Wolff's liaison assignment affect him physically? Were his efforts to shorten the war in Europe successful?

☞ **Q 44.**

Was Hitler's program to annex the European part of the Soviet Union to the Third Reich based on his fear and hatred of Communism or his demand that the mineral wealth of the Soviet Union become Nazi Germany's?

☞ **Q 45.**

Have gliders ever been used in a military operation during a war? If so, what was the first and most impressive operation of this kind?

☞ **Q 46.**

Who was the first American general to go into battle on French soil after the Allied invasion of the European continent in June 1944?

☞ **Q 47.**

Prinsengracht 263 is one of the most famous addresses from World War II. Why is this address so significant? Hint: A discovery there in 1944 made the address a tourist attraction several years after the war, and it remains one today.

WORLD WAR II AND THE NAZIS

☞ Q 48.

What was Hitler supposed to have replied when asked how he thought he could get away with the murder of six million Jews?

☞ Q 49.

Two events of historical significance occurred on December 7, 1941. What are they? Two little hints: The answer to one can be found on the third largest island of the state of Hawaii, the other in Kulm.

☞ Q 50.

Did Winston Churchill's wartime cabinet know exactly when and where Adolf Hitler was going to start his *blitzkrieg* offensive against Holland, France, and Belgium in 1940?

☞ Q 51.

In 1987, the "Butcher of Lyon," Klaus Barbie (1913–91), who had been head of the German Gestapo in the south of France, was tried in France for wartime crimes against humanity. Almost forty years before his trial, the American Counter-Intelligence Corps made it possible for the war criminal to flee to South America. He had supplied the Americans with some information about Communist activities in Europe. What was the most ironic aspect of this outrageous policy?

QUESTIONS

☞ Q 52.

There was a European country which was a cobelligerent of Nazi Germany in World War II. Why did the U.S. government never declare war on this country and only break diplomatic relations with it several weeks after the Allies had landed on the European continent on D day in June 1944?

☞ Q 53.

After England's Prime Minister Neville Chamberlain (1869–1940) had flown to Germany three times to meet Hitler in 1938 to discuss Germany's takeover of Czech-controlled Sudetenland, the English leader was celebrated for his policy of appeasement, but he was also criticized. What was the cynical ditty he frequently heard for his appeasing Hitler? And how did Hitler feel about gaining the Sudetenland without a battle? Was there another territorial winner after the Munich agreement?

☞ Q 54.

Which country saved the highest percentage of European Jews from the German Nazi occupation forces? Can you name three other European countries that did their best to boycott Hitler's anti-Semitic deportation laws?

☞ Q 55.

Is it true that the Soviet Union never showed any gratitude to the Allies, who risked, and often lost, their lives supplying the Soviet Union with arms after Hitler invaded the Soviet Union in 1941? If it is not true, how did the Soviets show their gratitude?

☞ **Q 56.**

What country declared war on the Western Allies *and* on Nazi Germany in World War II?

☞ **Q 57.**

What country that declared war on the United States, on January 25, 1942, did the United States refuse to declare war on in return? Why?

☞ **Q 58.**

Which day of the year will always be associated with three of the leading historical figures of World War II: Churchill, Hitler, and Roosevelt?

☞ **Q 59.**

When informed by President Truman of the successful explosion of the first nuclear device in New Mexico in 1945, how did Winston Churchill react to this earth-shattering news?

☞ **Q 60.**

Of all the major Nazi war criminals, only one of them—the Jew-baiter Julius Streicher—groaned when he was hanged after the 1946 Nuremberg trials. Why?

☞ Q 61.

What event led President Roosevelt and the U.S. government to decide that America would continue assisting the British against Hitler after the fall of France in 1940?

☞ Q 62.

Did the Nazis ever give the International Red Cross permission to inspect their World War II concentration camps? If they did, how did the Red Cross help the concentration camp inmates?

☞ Q 63.

Where did the German Reichswehr and the future panzer general Heinz Guderian set up a secret aviation and armored-vehicle school in 1926?

☞ Q 64.

Name the one German Nazi who voluntarily spent some time in prison for a crime he did not commit.

☞ Q 65.

Name the exact date when Adolf Hitler was elected to head the German government.

WORLD WAR II AND THE NAZIS

☞ **Q 66.**

How can the League of Nations be held responsible for preventing the *Anschluss* between Germany and Austria when history has established that Hitler succeeded in the 1938 *Anschluss* and united the two nations?

☞ **Q 67.**

Did Hitler ever intervene to prevent a Jew from being sent to a death camp during World War II?

☞ **Q 68.**

Name the city with the largest surviving Jewish population in Nazi-occupied Europe at the end of World War II and the reason for the high concentration of Jews there.

☞ **Q 69.**

Were some German Jews members of the Nazi sports team during Hitler's Olympic Games in Berlin in 1936? If this is not the case, how did this rumor originate? If German Jews participated in the games, what were the results?

☞ **Q 70.**

Who said in 1940 that he had nothing to offer to the British people but "blood, sweat, and tears"?

QUESTIONS

☞ **Q 71.**

Which honorary title did the Nazis confer on *Der Rosenkavalier*'s composer, Richard Strauss?

☞ **Q 72.**

Can it be proven that the three Baltic republics—Estonia, Latvia, and Lithuania—willingly accepted Soviet rule after Hitler occupied neighboring Poland in September 1939? And what was the one earth-shattering consequence of this Soviet occupation?

☞ **Q 73.**

According to President Truman's handwritten journal, intercepted messages revealed that as early as June 1945 Emperor Hirohito wanted to terminate Japanese participation in World War II. A U.S. intelligence study, discovered in the National Archives in 1989, concluded that on August 9, 1945, Japanese Premier Suzuki presented the emperor with the alternative of either fighting an impossible war or surrendering. What event caused the Japanese cabinet to suggest to the emperor that they lay down their arms? And why did a single word in July 1945 help to change the history of the world?

☞ **Q 74.**

The Nazis accused the Jews of dominating the medical profession in Germany before Hitler came to power in

1933. Before 1933, what percentage of medical doctors in Germany were Jewish?

☞ **Q 75.**

Which Nazi made the following observation: "Whenever I hear the word *culture,* I reach for my revolver"?

☞ **Q 76.**

Hitler never voluntarily abandoned territory to the enemy. True or false? If false, when did he do so?

☞ **Q 77.**

Has it ever been established if there was a person who was a diehard Nazi to the very end, yet who had been willing to surrender the German armed forces along the entire western front to the Allies before 1945?

☞ **Q 78.**

What was the best-kept secret of the builder of Germany's Nazi Luftwaffe?

☞ **Q 79.**

The reputed father of the Nazi gas chambers, a Gestapo department chief, head of the German criminal police, and ex-commander of a dreaded *Einsatzgruppe* (mobile death squad), Artur Nebe was finally captured and executed. When and by whom?

QUESTIONS

☞ Q 80.

Where was the last official seat of government and capital of the Third Reich, and what internal governmental conflict virtually overshadowed Nazi Germany's surrender to the Allies as far as the last Nazi administrators were concerned?

POLITICAL WORLD

☞ **Q 1.**

Which two of the following countries did their best not to send escaping Jews back to Nazi Germany during World War II: Cuba, Japan, Switzerland, Spain, Portugal, the Soviet Union (before Hitler's invasion in 1941), and the United States (before Pearl Harbor)?

☞ **Q 2.**

When James Madison (1751–1836) served as a representative in the first Congress, was he a Republican or a Democrat?

☞ **Q 3.**

In 1986, President Reagan compared his secret weapons sales to Iran with President Franklin D. Roosevelt's des-

QUESTIONS

troyer deal with Winston Churchill during World War II. Was he justified in making this comparison?

☞ Q 4.

What was the original purpose of the division of Korea at the 38th parallel in September 1945?

☞ Q 5.

What do the constitutions of Mexico and Germany's old Weimar Republic have in common?

☞ Q 6.

What political event led to the Balfour Declaration (November 2, 1917), which promised to establish a national home for the Jewish people in Palestine?

☞ Q 7.

Who first administered the granting of patents under the U.S. Constitution? And how many of his own patents did this administrator take out in the U.S. Patent Office for his inventions?

☞ Q 8.

In the 19th century, why did the U.S. government encourage American Indians to eat their favorite food?

POLITICAL WORLD

☞ **Q 9.**

Was John Quincy Adams (1767–1848) right in maintaining in 1828 that Andrew Jackson (1767–1845) was an adulterer and a bigamist?

☞ **Q 10.**

How much of a trick question is it when somebody asks if there was a legitimately established Soviet republic inside the western part of Germany?

☞ **Q 11.**

White supremacists claim that blacks have never had the franchise in South Africa because they are by nature unfit to vote in a white man's world. Can any of this be proven wrong to the white racists?

☞ **Q 12.**

Madame Tussaud's wax museum in London had two wax figures created in the likenesses of which two conflicting citizens of South Africa? How did the public react to seeing figures of such diverse and opposing points of view?

☞ **Q 13.**

Which country had never had an election in its 2,500-year history until 1987?

QUESTIONS

☞ **Q 14.**

When President Woodrow Wilson (1856–1924) was incapacitated by a stroke in October 1919, his wife, Edith Bolling Galt Wilson, became the principal caretaker of the president's business for about six weeks, until Mr. Wilson could resume his duties more fully. If a similar situation should arise today, how much can the determined wife of an incapacitated president succeed in controlling the flow of policy papers and letters to his sickroom and consulting with Cabinet members the way Mrs. Wilson did after World War I?

☞ **Q 15.**

What caused members of the White House staff in the early 1970s to set up the White House "plumbers," the ones who later broke into the Democratic National Committee headquarters at the Watergate office complex?

☞ **Q 16.**

Who called whom "the nearest thing to a human machine"?

☞ **Q 17.**

Nixon helped to organize a labor union and in 1955 was instrumental in bailing a woman out of jail after a history-making racial incident. True or false?

POLITICAL WORLD

☞ **Q 18.**

After the U.S. Congress vetoed any further American aid to help the contras overthrow the Communist Sandinista regime in Nicaragua, why was no legislation introduced to curtail or forbid U.S. military intervention in countries now under Communist rule?

☞ **Q 19.**

Is there an instance on record when more medals were granted by the military than the actual number of troops that participated in the military campaign?

☞ **Q 20.**

Who was the only political candidate in the last hundred years or so to jump directly from the U.S. House of Representatives (although he had just been elected to the Senate) into the Oval Office at the White House?

☞ **Q 21.**

Who was the bisexual national leader about whom it was said that he was the perfect husband to every woman and the perfect wife to every man?

☞ **Q 22.**

Which member of the House of Representatives was known mainly for being the father of a famous daughter?

QUESTIONS

☞ **Q 23.**

Besides being related and becoming presidents of the United States, what else do Theodore Roosevelt and Franklin Delano Roosevelt have in common?

☞ **Q 24.**

George Washington was known to have blessed a youngster with a pat on the head in 1789, when the boy was six years old. Who was that youngster, who would become famous in his own right, and what else did he have in common with the Founding Father?

☞ **Q 25.**

A plaque can still be found on the moon with the name of a famous politician inscribed on it. What name is engraved on the plaque that was deliberately left behind by an astronaut?

☞ **Q 26.**

How many presidents of the United States could boast of a budget surplus and no public debt?

☞ **Q 27.**

What was the greatest failing of the U.S. ambassador to Japan just prior to World War II?

POLITICAL WORLD

☞ **Q 28.**

In the 1980s, the United States traded the most with which part of the world?

☞ **Q 29.**

What were three very important (but rarely mentioned) causes of the Depression of the 1920s and the 1929 crash?

☞ **Q 30.**

Which country had both U.S. and Soviet military installations with American and Soviet personnel within its areal borders?

☞ **Q 31.**

What president of the United States was baptized Leslie King?

☞ **Q 32.**

Who was the first person to use the phrase "cold war"?

☞ **Q 33.**

When Nazi war criminal Klaus Barbie was judged after his 1987 trial in Lyon, the French jury and judges had to answer 341 specific questions about his guilt. To 340

QUESTIONS

questions, they said yes. To the last question, they answered no. Why did the jury and judge weaken on this sole question of guilt about the "Butcher of Lyon"?

☞ **Q 34.**

In the history of the United States, when did three presidents serve in the White House during the same year, and who were they?

☞ **Q 35.**

When did a twentieth-century American president thank an artist for trying to keep the United States out of a war?

☞ **Q 36.**

What was the literary work that influenced the U.S. Supreme Court in its 1954 ruling that segregation in public schools was unconstitutional? Hint: The author, whose epoch-making book appeared in 1944, won the Nobel Prize in economics in 1974; his wife won a Nobel Prize eight years later for her efforts to promote world disarmament.

☞ **Q 37.**

After the Northwest Ordinance of 1787 was passed by the new Congress of the United States, any area east of the Mississippi River could draw up a constitution when the population there reached a total of 60,000. Once this local constitution had been approved by

Congress, that part of the territory could become a state, as Kentucky did, for instance. Each new state had the same rights and powers as the original thirteen states, such as to create its own policy toward slavery, establish its own public schools, and offer its settlers the right to attend the church of their choice. There is one thing wrong with the above statement. Can you pick it out?

☞ **Q 38.**

Who made the following observations about the Constitution just after it had been framed by the Constitutional Convention at Independence Hall in Philadelphia? 1) He said, "It is frail and worthless." 2) This delegate was opposed to any idea of "weaving into the Constitution a respect for wealth." 3) This man expressed his dislike of anything that worked to "lower the common people."

☞ **Q 39.**

Which anti-Semitic group at the turn of the century was financially based on the profits made by the founder's father, whose source of affluence can be traced solely to his Jewish employer?

☞ **Q 40.**

William O'Dwyer (1890–1964) resigned as mayor of New York on September 1, 1950, to accept the assignment as U.S. ambassador to Mexico. Under the New York City charter, he was succeeded by the president of the city council, Vincent R. Impellitteri (1900–87), and Impellitteri won an election to the post in November 1950. What was the most remarkable thing about his election victory?

☞ **Q 41.**

Do American government administrations discriminate exclusively against left-wingers when blocking foreigners' entrance into the United States?

☞ **Q 42.**

After several futile attempts to overthrow Henry VII (1457–1509) were made, the king called into being the Star Chamber Act of 1487 to deal promptly with riots and crimes. Does the reputation of these tribunals' proceeding with arbitrary and unfair strong-arm methods derive from the Star Chamber Act of 1487?

☞ **Q 43.**

On May Day 1960, what startling secret message was conveyed to Soviet Premier Nikita Khrushchev (1894–1971) as he stood on the viewers' rostrum atop the Lenin mausoleum overlooking Red Square in Moscow, watching the annual military parade?

☞ **Q 44.**

Why are private schools in England actually referred to as "public" schools?

☞ **Q 45.**

Who wrote and published viciously anti-Semitic articles in his weekly *Dearborn Independent*—articles that are still in print today as a book titled *The International Jew*?

☞ **Q 46.**

Which president of the United States made the following statement in an appeal to Congress concerning a road bill and swore to veto it if it passed in both the House and the Senate: "Have you looked at the condition of the treasury, at the appropriations already made by Congress, at the amount of their unavoidable claims upon it"?

☞ **Q 47.**

Did anybody write the "I have a dream" speech for Dr. Martin Luther King, Jr., or did he prepare the speech himself?

☞ **Q 48.**

How many press secretaries did President Ronald Reagan have while in the White House?

☞ **Q 49.**

Which two belligerents of World War II (1939–45) are still at war, and why?

QUESTIONS

☞ **Q 50.**

Which historical document, political essay, patriotic address, congressional edict, presidential decree, or words penned by the Founding Fathers first cited the Pledge of Allegiance to the flag of the United States?

☞ **Q 51.**

Which twentieth-century leader made the following statement about another twentieth-century leader: "I got the impression that here was a man who could be relied upon when he had given his word"?

☞ **Q 52.**

Which head of state rejected pressure to appoint a certain person as minister of defense because it might have annoyed a foreign leader?

☞ **Q 53.**

Which twentieth-century United States president made the following statement: "The misuse of cocaine is undoubtedly an American habit, the most threatening of the drug habits that has ever appeared in this country"?

☞ **Q 54.**

During the 1940 election campaign in the United States, one of the parties running against the Republican,

POLITICAL WORLD

Willkie, and the Democratic incumbent, Roosevelt, was the Surprise party. Who ran for president on that ticket?

☞ **Q 55.**

Which American president wrote a famous speech on the back of an envelope?

☞ **Q 56.**

Which American first exhorted people to move west by proclaiming: "Go west, young man"?

PLACES

☞ Q 1.

It is no secret that the Protestant reformer John Calvin was born in 1509 in the Picardy province of France. Yet he labored for most of his adult life in Geneva, a city where he was received with the greatest enthusiasm. He recodified the Genevan laws and constitution and was consulted on every affair involving religion, the economy, trade, and the police that came before the city council. Today he is referred to as the great Swiss reformer. Is it known why and when Calvin renounced his French nationality and became a naturalized Swiss citizen?

☞ Q 2.

What did American aviator James Angel rediscover in 1935 while exploring Venezuela by air, which appeared decades later in the *Guinness Book of World Records*?

PLACES

☞ **Q 3.**

What country is 1,300 miles long, with examples of completely different vegetation at each of its ends, yet whose total land area is smaller in square miles than the American state of Montana?

☞ **Q 4.**

Between 1612 and 1630 a British tailor named Robert Baker made his fortune creating and selling turnover collars that were fashionable at the time. When he retired, he built himself a house and called it by the name of these collars. The name stuck and it later became one of London's most famous sight-seeing attractions. What is the name of this tourist spot?

☞ **Q 5.**

The Langebro and the Knippelsbro join the islands of Sjaelland and Amager. What capital was built on these islands, parts of which have been inhabited for 6,000 years?

☞ **Q 6.**

The Spanish town of Jeréz de la Frontera has been the center for what type of industry for over 3,000 years?

☞ **Q 7.**

The people of Granada, Spain, claim that the Alhambra, the gigantic Moorish palace, is the eighth wonder of the world. Where did the word *Alhambra* actually originate, and what does it signify?

☞ Q 8.

In what way has Runnymede often been referred to as a place that has benefited the common people? Where exactly is Runnymede located?

☞ Q 9.

When and where did Christopher Columbus (1451–1506) land the three times he visited the New World? On which of these voyages did he land in what today is the continental United States?

☞ Q 10.

Why did Sir Christopher Wren and Robert Hooks decide that the monument they designed in London to commemorate the Great Fire of 1666 should be exactly 202 feet (62 meters) high? And what lie was first recorded on the column's pedestal by order of King Charles II?

☞ Q 11.

One of the best-known images in all recorded history is supposed to be in the likeness of someone called Chephren. It also guards Chephren's remains. What is this image called today?

PLACES

☞ **Q 12.**

When the poet William Wordsworth (1770–1850) composed the poem "Lines Composed a Few Miles Above Tintern Abbey," he wrote about the twelfth-century Cistercian abbey on the river Wey. Up to 1974 the abbey was part of an English county, but then it was ceded to another country. To which country was it ceded, and what is the new name of the county in which the abbey is located?

☞ **Q 13.**

The construction of which English cathedral took four hundred years to complete?

☞ **Q 14.**

Which city is expected to be the most densely populated urban area by the year 2000?

☞ **Q 15.**

How many of the world's (approximately) 5½ billion people in the 1990s live in developing countries? And in the year 2000, how many people will be living in Asia?

☞ **Q 16.**

Why did Berlin's architecture before World War II resemble residential apartment houses in Paris?

QUESTIONS

☞ **Q 17.**

In which city has Benjamin Franklin (1706–90) been compared to a pregnant oyster?

☞ **Q 18.**

About 50,000 Arawak Indians, who came from the Amazon basin in South America, led a peaceful agricultural life on an island they called Boriquén for 600 years before the Spaniards arrived in 1493 and seized the Indians and their island in the name of Ferdinand V and Isabella I. The Spaniards forced them and the black slaves the Spaniards imported from Africa to pay gold in tribute to Spain and then be converted to Christianity. In the meantime, the Spaniards renamed the island, calling it what?

☞ **Q 19.**

It is a huge, almost uninhabited territory. Over a period of nearly a century, beginning in 1770, more than 160,000 convicts—men and women, a quarter of them Irish—were shipped to places called Van Diemen's Land, Moreton Bay, and Norfolk Island. Many of them were killed by their own compatriots, or by other settlers, and in retaliation they tortured and killed those native to the distant land. What is this distant land, which today has become a center of great attraction for tourists and legal immigrants desirous of sharing the rich life of its residents?

PLACES

☞ **Q 20.**

Which world-famous woman helped the Allied war effort by identifying Nazi sympathizers in her native country?

☞ **Q 21.**

A quartet of questions regarding one of the most famous waterways in the world—the Panama Canal: 1) How long is the canal and how many ships traverse it on the average every year? 2) Each time a ship passes through the canal, how many gallons of water must be pumped into the locks and where is the water taken from? 3) What happens to the water that has been pumped into the locks? 4) Can you figure out which single word in these three questions does not apply to the Panama Canal?

☞ **Q 22.**

What was the nickname given to people who were so greedy for land they paid no heed to time and law?

☞ **Q 23.**

A sprawling Portuguese settlement with about 460,000 inhabitants has had some of the finest Portuguese architecture for over four centuries, yet only 20 percent of the population speaks Portuguese. How can this be explained?

QUESTIONS

☞ **Q 24.**

There is a river in Cambridge, England, whose banks have been a site of relaxation for Alfred Tennyson, Rupert Brooke, and Sir Isaac Newton. Chaucer set one of his bawdy stories in the *Canterbury Tales* on its banks. Lord Byron used to go there for a swim on summer afternoons. Even a literary magazine, started the year Charlie Chaplin was born (1889), was named after it. What is the name of this river in Cambridge?

☞ **Q 25.**

In 1911, the Norwegian explorer Roald Amundsen (1872–1928) wintered there. Seventeen years later, what American naval aviator went there in the *City of New York* and established a shore station, which by 1935 had become America's biggest, most elaborate expedition base ever erected in that region? And what is the shore station?

☞ **Q 26.**

Skyscrapers built in the twentieth century are the tallest buildings ever. When were the largest and tallest buildings erected in North America prior to the end of the nineteenth century, and who built them?

☞ **Q 27.**

In the 1970s, Connolly Str. 31 made world headlines for a couple of days. What happened there for two harrowing days that is remembered with great horror every few years because the whole world watched this tragedy on television?

☞ Q 28.

What is the second-largest French-speaking city in the world, which is surrounded by water and also boasts huge harbor facilities?

☞ Q 29.

Uncle Tom in the novel *Uncle Tom's Cabin* was a black slave. Which city named a subway station in the black man's honor?

☞ Q 30.

Which train has been leaving the same station for the same destination at the same time every weekday for over one hundred years?

☞ Q 31.

Rome wasn't built in a day, but at least it was founded only once. Can you name one of the world's capitals that was founded not once, but twice? What was the reason for this double ceremony?

☞ Q 32.

In June 1885 the United States imported something from Europe that was worth about a quarter of a million dollars and helped to enlighten the world. What was it? And why was the import less expensive than its accessories?

☞ **Q 33.**

In 1846, Edgar Allan Poe (1809–49) left Manhattan and moved to the country, a hilly section of New York State, not far from St. John's College, known for its salubrious air. Exactly where did Poe move to, and what is the name of St. John's College today?

☞ **Q 34.**

Who designed a home for Alexander Hamilton two years before Hamilton's death, and what other famous building is this architect credited with designing? Where was Hamilton's last house?

☞ **Q 35.**

At the turn of the twentieth century, who were the two men who conducted an experiment on the grass of Huffman Prairie, Ohio, a half-mile-long field on the Dayton-Springfield trolley line, which two years later became a successful experiment in the South, lasting twelve seconds, and changed the course of history?

☞ **Q 36.**

Situated between Norrland and Götaland, this settlement has witnessed fifteen hundred years of history: first as a religious capital of the Norsemen, then as a political capital for a Christian see, and finally as an educational stronghold. What is the name of this place whose kings united the country under one crown?

☞ **Q 37.**

Since the twelfth century, Portugal has been the world's largest producer of what natural product? Hint: The natural product can be removed from its source only once every nine years.

☞ **Q 38.**

Which two cities are connected by the longest suspension bridge in Europe, completed in 1966? Hint: It crosses the Tejo.

☞ **Q 39.**

Where is the "White Spider," a place that is not usually found on any map? Hint: It is one of the few places not considered a popular tourist attraction in Central Europe, although colorful pictures of it look very inviting.

☞ **Q 40.**

What country has three national capitals?

☞ **Q 41.**

Ecuadoreans call it Archipiélago de Colón. Charles Darwin described it as "lost in time." The rest of the world has another name for this archipelago on the equator. What does the name mean in English, and why was it given this name?

☞ Q 42.

Over two hundred years ago there was a man whose profession related to his name. He was also the first man to establish a settlement on the site where America's third most populous city is located today. Who was he and what job did he have?

☞ Q 43.

What kind of stone is the Great Pyramid made of, how many blocks were needed to build it, and how much does each block weigh?

☞ Q 44.

What is the world's most frequently visited museum?

☞ Q 45.

In which country were only 30 percent of the population citizens? Is there another country with even fewer citizens among its population?

☞ Q 46.

Which country has had about 190 rulers in the last century and a half? Hint: The country has the highest infant-mortality rate in the world.

PLACES

☞ **Q 47.**

The Apennines can be found in Italy, the Caucasus Mountains in southeast Europe, the Alps in Austria, France, Italy, the former Yugoslavia, and Switzerland. But where can other mountain ranges that bear the same names also be found?

☞ **Q 48.**

What do the following geographical names have in common: Berlin, Wellington, Winchester, Panama, Inverness, Holland, Toledo, and Hamburg?

☞ **Q 49.**

What one place in the United States interested Sigmund Freud? Hint: It's full of wheels and, like Freud's patients, it's full of ups and downs.

☞ **Q 50.**

What did the African nations of Liberia and Ethiopia (formerly Abyssinia) have in common before World War I?

☞ **Q 51.**

In which country are three out of four citizens still illiterate and make only the equivalent of $80 a year, yet there are popular attractions, the Potala Palace and the Jokhang Temple, as well as the busy Barkhor market?

QUESTIONS

☞ **Q 52.**

Do you know the name of the man who did the interior engineering for the Statue of Liberty and also designed a monument for the Paris Exposition of 1889?

☞ **Q 53.**

In New Amsterdam, the Dutch referred to one of the localities as "Krom Moerasje," which, in English, means "little crooked swamp." What is the place known as today?

☞ **Q 54.**

One capital outside the United States was named after an American citizen. Who was so honored, and what is the name of the capital?

☞ **Q 55.**

While the People's Republic of China is making giant strides in the fields of agricultural and industrial production, is it now surpassing most countries in its dairy output?

☞ **Q 56.**

Which state in New England did not border on another New England state, yet was part of it?

PLACES

☞ **Q 57.**

Henry IV was the Holy Roman Emperor and king of the Germans from 1056 to 1106. Another Henry IV (Henry of Lancaster) was the king of England from 1399 to 1413. Still another Henry IV was the first of France's Bourbon kings and ruled from 1589 to 1610. Which state in the United States was named after a grandson of one of the above three kings? Who was the grandson?

☞ **Q 58.**

Has it ever been established who made the nickname for New York City, the "Big Apple," widely known?

☞ **Q 59.**

Which part of Boston was at one time called Mount Whoredom?

☞ **Q 60.**

According to the Census Bureau for International Research, by the year 2055, which country will most likely become the world's fastest growing nation after Mexico and India?

☞ **Q 61.**

One place in Europe not only saw some of the fiercest fighting of World War II, but was also the birthplace and vacation resort of two emperors. What is the name of the place and who were the emperors? A hint: The emperors are known for their enduring infamy.

☞ Q 62.

Percentage-wise, how much space does the United States (without Alaska) occupy on the earth's surface? 8 percent? 11 percent? Even more? Or less?

☞ Q 63.

For obvious reasons the Bolsheviks renamed Petrograd Leningrad in 1924, but why did they change the name of the town Ekaterinburg to Sverdlovsk in the same year?

☞ Q 64.

What is the only private residence in existence with its own court of justice and eleven prison cells?

☞ Q 65.

In which well-known location is a misquotation from Shakespeare's *The Tempest* engraved in stone?

☞ Q 66.

Which church does Charles Dickens describe in *Our Mutual Friend* with the following words: "a very hideous church with four towers at the corners, generally

PLACES

resembling some petrified monster, frightful and gigantic, on its back with legs in the air"?

☞ Q 67.

A number of politicians have been tried and convicted at London's Old Bailey. What two things are unique about its bronze figure, the Lady of Justice, on the Central Criminal Court's dome?

☞ Q 68.

Although the highest outdoor statue in London measures 212 feet (65 meters) from the ground to the top, why can Admiral Lord Nelson's statue in London's Trafalgar Square, which only stands 170 feet (51.82 meters) from street level, also be considered the highest outdoor statue in London?

☞ Q 69.

Not too long ago mass demonstrations by students, radicals, and workers in many countries helped change the political face of Europe. Of the following, can you name the one country or city that did not participate in these rebellions: Hungary and other Balkan countries; Berlin, Leipzig, and many German cities; Poland; Russia; Czechoslovakia; Austria; and France?

☞ Q 70.

Who ruled Moscow for the most part of 1605 to 1606 and 1610 to 1611, and where did these rulers meet their ignoble ends?

QUESTIONS

☞ **Q 71.**

Although not very popular because of her conservative Catholic practices, she is credited with having introduced marmalade, tea, and the fork to England three centuries ago. And because of her colonial connections a place in the United States was named in her honor. Who was she? Where was she born? And where is the place named for her in the United States?

☞ **Q 72.**

What is ironic about the name of one of the most bitterly contested Civil War battles, fought about one hundred miles southwest of Nashville, Tennessee, in April 1862 and costing the North and the South each about 25 percent of their troops?

RELIGION

☞ **Q 1.**

How can the popular Pope John XXIII be considered an antipope? And what did he have in common with Pope Benedict XIII?

☞ **Q 2.**

To whom can these words be ascribed: "The Jews are the best blood on earth. Through them alone the Holy Ghost wished to give all the books of the Holy Scripture to the world"?

☞ **Q 3.**

What person urged that all synagogues and books and houses of Jews be burned? He personally wished that he could destroy all Jews with hellfire, considering them children of the Devil—"thirsty bloodhounds and a plague." He furthermore advised that one should deal with Jews mercilessly—"their tongues torn out through the back of their necks."

☞ **Q 4.**

What caused Martin Luther to turn from an admirer of Jews into a vicious anti-Semite?

☞ **Q 5.**

Did Theodor Herzl's idea for a new Jewish homeland result in a standing ovation for him at the Zionist International Congress at Basle when he addressed the congress for the last time, shortly before his death?

☞ **Q 6.**

Between 1890 and 1910, the teachings of what man culminated in creating a new mecca for mankind, resulting in multitudes traveling to visit him? A hint: He was probably the most venerated man in the world at the time.

☞ **Q 7.**

Why has the Catholic church always maintained that abortion is a mortal sin? And how did Saint Thomas Aquinas (c. 1226–74) feel about the Church's stand against it?

RELIGION

☞ **Q 8.**

In World War I, he served as a U-boat commander, sinking many Allied ships. About twenty years later, in 1937, he was arrested and spent almost eight years in the concentration camps of Sachsenhausen and Dachau. Who was this German, and what happened to him later?

☞ **Q 9.**

How can dogmatism best be described in terms of religious belief? And why does a dogma take root in the human mind?

☞ **Q 10.**

Where does the word *dharma* come from? What does it mean to a Brahman, to a Buddhist, and to a Hindu?

☞ **Q 11.**

What Marseilles-born graphic artist occasionally directed anticlerical gibes at the Jesuits and the Capuchins in the nineteenth century? A hint: Although he produced a thousand woodcut designs, he was also known for his religious paintings.

☞ **Q 12.**

How true is it that Lucrezia Borgia (the Duchess of Ferrara) lived a life of debauchery?

QUESTIONS

☞ **Q 13.**

Why did history, starting with Machiavelli (1469–1527), accuse the Spanish Borgia family of every foul crime under the sun?

☞ **Q 14.**

The Roman Catholic church assailed the Protestant Reformation movement in Europe; did the Jews fare better at the hands of the popes after Martin Luther's death?

☞ **Q 15.**

When the law stating that Swedes could only leave the established church of Sweden if they decided to join another "foreign religious community" was rescinded in 1952, was there a mass exodus from the Lutheran faith?

☞ **Q 16.**

The only times a pope has been arrested were when Herod Agrippa I (10 B.C.–A.D. 44) imprisoned Saint Peter, and Charles V had Clement VII removed from Rome (1527–28). True or false?

☞ **Q 17.**

Were the powerful spokespersons of the black liberation movement in the United States happy with Dr. Martin Luther King's pronouncements the last few years of his life?

RELIGION

☞ Q 18.

Did the demoralizing consequences of the Reformation and Counter-Reformation induce Pope Leo X (1475–1521) to continue the sale of indulgences?

☞ Q 19.

What strand of philosophical spiritualism can be detected in Pindar's *Olympians II* and later in Plato, who interpreted it in his *Republic* and *Phaedo*? Lucian and Menander and especially Ennius made reference to it in Roman literature, while the Jewish religion adopted it in the Cabala. The Manichaeans and Giordano Bruno revived it, while Goethe and Lessing played with it in German literature. What is this common strand?

☞ Q 20.

Creationists insist that Eve was the first woman and the mother of the human race, and twentieth-century biologists agree with the religious fundamentalists. True or false?

☞ Q 21.

What is the official state religion in Italy?

☞ Q 22.

What is ironical about the original burial place of the Christian reformer who died about a hundred years before the birth of Martin Luther?

QUESTIONS

☞ **Q 23.**

Can you name the country that follows three sacred teachings today by which to live? Hint: One of the three religions, or ways of life, derives its name from the language of another country. The second religion has the greatest number of followers. The third has the greatest influence on its adherents.

☞ **Q 24.**

When Pontius Pilate asked the leaders of the Jewish people in the Judgment Hall whether Christ or Bar-Abbas, a man who had stirred up a revolt against the Roman Empire, should be crucified, the leaders told the Roman governor of Jerusalem to save the life of Jesus, and he was not crucified. What is wrong with this statement?

☞ **Q 25.**

A camel was directly responsible for helping to create the most important date in one of the world's major religions. Or was it another animal?

☞ **Q 26.**

What caused the Jews in the sixth century B.C. to believe that there was only one God, that Heaven and Hell awaited humans after life, and that a Messiah would one day bring happiness to the world?

RELIGION

☞ **Q 27.**

To which historical events can we attribute the fact that the four Gospels absolved the Romans of any responsibility in Christ's death and made scapegoats of Jews for the crucifixion?

☞ **Q 28.**

In which sect can an angel called Moroni be found? What was the consequence of Moroni's sudden appearance and the fate of the man who saw him?

☞ **Q 29.**

If you were told that the Islamic religion was closer to Christianity than to Judaism, would you consider this to be a true assessment?

☞ **Q 30.**

The Moslems make their pilgrimage to Mecca in order to worship the Temple of the Black Stone, the Kaaba, and the Well of Ishmael, which were built to honor the prophet Mohammed (570–632). It is the place of his birth and the city where he was always respected and worshiped. How much of this is true, how much false?

☞ **Q 31.**

When the Muslims tumbled the Byzantine strongholds in Carthage, Tangiers, and Tripoli in the eighth century and crossed into Spain, the Arabic name of God was corrupted by the Spaniards and ended up as what?

☞ **Q 32.**

What is the title of the book that predicts the story of Jesus returning to earth, marrying, dying a natural death, and being buried, heralding the Day of Judgment?

☞ **Q 33.**

Where is it written that one should enter the clean part of a house with the right foot first, and an unclean place, such as a bathroom, with the left foot first?

☞ **Q 34.**

What do the following people have in common: Charles Taze Russell, George Fox, Ann Lee, Margaret and Kate Fox, Emanuel Swedenborg, William Miller, and Thomas Campbell?

☞ **Q 35.**

The sacred teachings of which sage are followed by about 400 million adherents throughout the world, including Protestants, Buddhists, Taoists, and Catholics? Hint: He once was a minister of crime.

☞ **Q 36.**

Death, war, sinfulness, famine, and pestilence are combined, except for one of the above, in the Judeo-Christian religions. What is the exception?

☞ **Q 37.**

In which religion are the initials "A. H." of overwhelming importance, and what do they signify?

☞ **Q 38.**

How is it possible that a Roman poet known to be a heathen is even now closely associated with Heaven?

☞ **Q 39.**

Which religious person is identified with a tree, and what does it signify?

☞ **Q 40.**

Why did a writer burn his poems in 1868 when he entered the Jesuit novitiate at Roehampton, near London? And why did the rector of Saint Beuno's Seminary in North Wales encourage the poet in December 1875 to write his first poem since becoming a Jesuit—a poem that became a masterpiece of English literature?

☞ **Q 41.**

When the three wise men were sent to Bethlehem by King Herod they followed the star in the east until it stood where the young child was with Mary, His mother. And they fell to the ground and worshiped Him and presented Him with gold and frankincense and myrrh. But they dreamed not to return to Herod and they departed into their own country another way. What is the one thing wrong with this summarized New Testament passage?

☞ **Q 42.**

Why did God choose the apple as the Forbidden Fruit on the Tree of Knowledge of Good and Evil, warning Adam and Eve not to eat that fruit?

☞ **Q 43.**

Thousands of years ago, which tribes were known collectively by the Egyptians as "Asiatics," and what was the principal reason that these tribes left Egypt for good around the thirteenth century B.C.?

☞ **Q 44.**

Exodus 12:37 claims: "The Israelites left Ramesses for Succoth, about six hundred thousand on the march—men, that is, not counting their families." Can this figure be considered accurate?

☞ **Q 45.**

Which detested dictator ordered the burning of the books of one of the greatest philosophers and spiritual and moral teachers of all time, yet had a country named after the place of his birth?

ANSWERS

GENERAL HISTORY

☞ **A 1.**

Adolf Hitler and Charlie Chaplin.

Hitler was born in Austria at 6 P.M., on Saturday, April 20, 1889.

Chaplin was born in England at 6 P.M., on Tuesday, April 16, 1889.

☞ **A 2.**

Both of them had relatives in the Swedish government during World War I. Dag's father, Hjalmar Hammarskjöld, was prime minister, and Raoul's uncle, K. A. Wallenberg, was his foreign minister. They served together from 1914 to 1917.

☞ **A 3.**

This was not the letter that convinced President Roosevelt to bring together the best scientists specializing in nuclear energy. The scientist who first thought of writing this letter was not Albert Einstein (1879–1955), but the Hungarian-born physicist Dr. Leo Szilard (1898–1964). It was Dr. Einstein's first letter, dated August 2, 1939, to President Roosevelt, a letter suggested by Dr. Szilard and twenty lines shorter than the one typed in October, that sparked the American effort to build the atomic bomb.

☞ **A 4.**

Because the wooden frigate *Merrimack* was fitted with iron plates and rechristened *Virginia* while still in dry dock before the battle on March 8 and 9, 1862. Both the crews of the *Virginia* and the *Monitor* lacked training. In fact, the smaller *Monitor* soon left the confrontation on the Elizabeth River, Virginia, to replenish its exhausted ammunition. When the Union's *Minnesota* ran aground on March 8, 1862, the *Virginia* inflicted heavier damage on her in the same fray. Soon after, the *Monitor*'s Captain Worden was blinded by iron splinters and his ship sheered into shallow water to change command. The *Virginia*'s Captain Jones thought he had won the battle and withdrew to lick his own wounds. The following day, March 9, at the Battle of Hampton Roads, near Norfolk, Virginia, the *Monitor* saved the day for the sorely pressed Union blockade fleet and decisively halted the bloody rampage begun the previous day. Designed by John Ericsson, the *Monitor* served as a prototype for all ironclads for another sixty years, until 1922. Ten months after the historic 1862 standoff with its Confederate counterpart, the *Monitor* sank in a storm near Cape Hatteras, North Carolina.

☞ A 5.

The fire did great damage to the *Normandie,* but in the final analysis the uncountable tons of water from the New York fire department and from an armada of tugs and fireboats caused the liner to roll over and settle in the muddy waters alongside Piers 88 and 90 on February 10, 1942. Three years later a local scrap dealer bought the destroyed ship for a mere $161,000.

☞ A 6.

Although this remark has always been ascribed to the Duke of Wellington (1769–1852) he could not have uttered it because there were no playing fields (or team sports) in Eton when he was a student there. In fact, he disliked Eton so much he refused to contribute money to a subscription drive for new buildings twenty-six years after he and Blücher (1742–1819) defeated Napoleon at Waterloo (1815). The so-called Wellington phrase was not coined until thirty-seven years after the Duke's death when Sir William Fraser combined remarks made by the Count of Montalembert and Sir Edward Creasy in their post-Wellington books in his 1889 book *Words on Wellington.*

☞ A 7.

On March 22, 1866, the first train robbery on the North American continent took place. The Reno brothers— John, Simeon, Bill, and Frank—and their gang stole $16,000 of gold, silver, and paper money. Immediately, an epidemic of train robberies began and a private detective, Allen Pinkerton, set out to bring the guilty to justice. In most cases he succeeded, and the Pinkertons were founded and are still operating today. Three of the Reno brothers were seized in 1868 and hanged in the New Albany, Indiana, jail. John Reno was in another jail at the time and after serving his sentence was never heard of again.

☞ **A 8.**

Hamilton and his two upstate colleagues could find no grounds for agreement among themselves, especially over what powers the new federal government should be given. Consequently, New York's delegation figured little in the debate.

☞ **A 9.**

The prime minister of Iceland, Olafur Johannesson, asked President Richard Nixon (b. 1913) and Secretary of State Henry Kissinger (b. 1923) to importune chess player Bobby Fischer (b. 1943) to attend the chess world championship in Reykjavik where Fischer's Soviet rival Boris Spassky (b. 1937) was already present during the opening ceremony on July 1, 1972. After a two-day postponement, Fischer showed up on July 4, 1972. The prize money was doubled, Fischer apologized to his opponent for his disrespectful behavior, then lost the first game to Spassky. Fischer did not show up for the second game, which he lost by default, but then scored five wins and three draws. Fischer didn't play chess again for twenty years, but even today most grandmasters consider him the greatest chess player of all time.

☞ A 10.

What incensed Aaron Burr and caused him to challenge Hamilton to a duel was a trivial remark that was reported to him as hearsay, namely that Hamilton allegedly had a "despicable" opinion of Burr. Hamilton died as a result of the duel the day afterward, on July 12, 1804, at age forty-nine. The irony was that on the very same spot where the duel was fought, Hamilton's eldest son had also fought a duel in 1801 and was killed.

☞ A 11.

Frederick the Great (Frederick II) (1712–86) spoke poorly in German but well in French. His palace, which he partly designed himself, was named Sanssouci (without sorrow) and built (1745–47) in Potsdam, near Berlin. It is now a tourist attraction that can be visited only by people who agree to wear specially designed felt slippers in the palace.

☞ A 12.

With his customary sangfroid, Danton eulogized the insurrection of May 31 and claimed that it had saved the republic. The following year Robespierre had him guillotined.

☞ A 13.

There was. The Russian general was Alexander Suvorov (1729–1800), one of the generals of the "Second Coalition" of 1798. He erased almost all the territorial gains made by Napoleon in Europe up to 1799, driving the

ANSWERS

French revolutionary army out of Italy in 1799. That same year, the Russian's victory was turned to defeat, and Suvorov returned in disgrace to Moscow, where he died the following year.

☞ A 14.

The real Thirty Years' Peace was concluded in 446 B.C. between the Athenians and Spartans. It also established Pericles's undisputed control of Athens' forces until 430 B.C.

☞ A 15.

France. In 1789, King Louis XVI (1754–93) acceded to the demands of the Third Estate—the bourgeoisie and the aristocratic faction among whom the egalitarian philosophy was most prevalent—and the emperor was compelled to convene the Estate General, the parliament, for the first time since it was called in 1614.

☞ A 16.

The act had neither racial nor moral implications. *Non-Intercourse* here meant the suspension by one country of commercial relations with another country. In 1809, President Madison used the act against Great Britain and France in retaliation for their violation of American neutral rights, particularly for their incitement of Indian hostilities in its western territory.

☞ A 17.

Sultan Suleiman I (sometimes II), the Magnificent, the greatest and most fortunate of sultans (c. 1495–1566).

The fruits of his campaigns were Aden, Algiers, Belgrade, Budapest, Tabriz, Baghdad, and Rhodes. He took part in thirteen of his campaigns. His treaty with France, directed against Charles V, lasted, with a few interruptions, over 350 years. Even today, some of his few misdeeds are still blamed on his Russian wife, known in the West as Roxelana.

☞ A 18.

Robespierre saw in the Reign of Terror a means to establish the ideal of Rousseau. Danton, on the other hand, ridiculed Robespierre's politico-religious projects. Robespierre felt that siding with Danton would prove to be a fatal association. He therefore decided in March 1794 to cooperate with the attackers in the Assembly and Convention on the Dantonites and their allies, the Hébertists. He proved to be right in this tactic, because a few days later the Hébertists and Danton were guillotined. However, Robespierre and his adherents were themselves considered outlaws by a tribunal four months later and immediately executed.

☞ A 19.

In the city of New York; the city of Washington did not exist at that time.

☞ A 20.

The Soviets proceeded to occupy the northern half of Korea on August 12, 1945—four days after Stalin had paid lip service to a free and independent Korea. The

ANSWERS

Americans did not reach South Korea until September 8, 1945. All Koreans, with the exception of the Communists, denounced the Soviets' plan to place Korea under a trusteeship for five years. Stalin, however, refused to budge and the Americans were forced to occupy the southern half of the country. In December 1945, a joint U.S.-U.S.S.R. commission was set up regarding a provisional Korean democratic government. This attempt failed when, by May 1946, the Soviet command prevented Korean groups from participating. A year later the zones had become a permanent fixture and unification became impossible.

☞ A 21.

Both of them were killed in duels. Pushkin was in his thirties; Hamilton in his forties.

☞ A 22.

On October 23, 1961, the prize was awarded posthumously to U.N. Secretary General Dag Hammarskjöld, who was killed in a plane accident in what was then Northern Rhodesia on September 18, 1961.

☞ A 23.

Thomas Paine (1737–1809).

☞ A 24.

No, it wasn't. In the first place, Hitler had never seized Moscow. Napoleon led his troops into the Russian capital. It was not so much the snow that defeated Hitler as the late-October rain that turned the nonexistent roads deep inside the Soviet Union into a quagmire of mud for the mechanized German forces and delayed their approach to Moscow. Napoleon's troops did not suffer from the cold in the Russian-scorched capital because they had left it already in October when the French presence there seemed senseless to Napoleon. It was only after both dictators had retreated from the vicinity of Moscow that the cold and the snow of Russia partly destroyed their armies.

☞ A 25.

Pericles (c. 490–429 B.C.) began the practice of paying jurors on a regular basis in 451 B.C.

☞ A 26.

Soviet foreign minister Maxim Litvinov, Soviet ambassador to the U.S., 1939–41. His views were never publicized during his life (1876–1951).

☞ A 27.

1) General Dwight D. Eisenhower (1890–1969), the supreme Allied commander in Europe. 2) Admiral William D. Leahy, chief of staff to President Truman and chairman of the Joint Chiefs of Staff. Both knew that a large-scale invasion of Japan by the United States on the scale of the Normandy invasion was never planned to take place, although as late as the end of July 1945 Admiral Raymond Spruance ordered his forces in Okinawa to prepare for an imminent attack

ANSWERS

on the Japanese mainland. President Truman in his memoirs quotes Admiral Leahy as having said about the atomic bomb: "That is the biggest fool thing we have ever done. The bomb will never go off." According to Truman, from the beginning, Leahy never got over his pique at being proven wrong about the nuclear weapon.

☞ A 28.

False. Although retreating on the western front, the German army to a large extent, at the moment of the November 1918 cease-fire, was far from defeated on the eastern front. It occupied part of Finland all the way south through Pskov-Orsha to an area south of the Soviet Union's Kursk and east of Rostov to the Don. Thus the Imperial Reich, in its dying moments, owned the Ukraine that was exacted from the Soviet Union at the Treaty of Brest-Litovsk (1918). It also occupied parts of the Crimea. Germany's aim was the perpetual subservience of the Soviet Union to the Reich, a policy Hitler tried to revive in 1941.

☞ A 29.

The Boers didn't solve it. In 1856, the Kaffirs were encouraged by their prophets to slaughter all their cattle, hoping that their heroes of old would return and drive out the white man. Instead, two-thirds of the population was deprived of food and died of starvation. The British later (1878) annexed all of Kaffraria, and the next year they made peace with the Zulus.

☞ A 30.

The 1516 law is still in effect, but fortunately it has nothing to do with the religious beliefs of Bavarian residents. It applies solely to the manufacture of beer which, the Duke ordered, should only be made of water, hops, malt, and yeast. Kölsch, the light, swiftly brewed beer of Cologne, still adheres to the "purity command."

☞ A 31.

The two troop carriers: the *Queen Mary* and the *Queen Elizabeth;* each of them weighed more than 83,000 gross tons. The record number of troops carried was on the *Queen Mary* in July 1943 when she transported 16,683 American troops to Scotland.

☞ A 32.

She was Rosa Luxemburg (1870–1919), who was a naturalized German. Actually she had emigrated in 1895 from Russian Poland, where she was born in 1870. Her radical antimilitarism caused her to be sentenced twice to prison terms and she spent most of World War I in protective custody. At one time she was the mistress, for five years, of Costya Zetkin—fifteen years her junior—the son of Germany's most famous feminist, Clara Zetkin. Rosa Luxemburg dismissed Frau Zetkin's feminist views as *meshugge.* She even dismissed Germany's rising anti-Semitism, frequently directed against her and her Communist Spartacus League colleague Karl Liebknecht (1871–1919), as unimportant. Both of them were arrested on January 15, 1919, during a work-

ANSWERS

ers' revolt and murdered by German army officers on the way to Berlin's Moabit prison. Her body was immediately thrown into the Landwehr Kanal and not recovered for four months.

☞ A 33.

Caligula (A.D. 12–41). His father, Germanicus, dressed him up as a soldier when Caligula was still a child, making him wear soldiers' boots, or *caligae*. That name stuck from the time he was six years old.

☞ A 34.

George Washington wrote this to his fellow Virginian Henry Lee near the close of the eighteenth century.

☞ A 35.

Not only did Ms. Banks join Dr. Martin Luther King, Jr. (1929–68) in marching through the streets of Atlanta, but later she became the top executive at Rich's, the very department store where she had been arrested. She was also the first African-American woman on the Atlanta City Council.

☞ A 36.

The American Civil War. These writers opposed the Mexican War but abandoned their humanitarian feelings when it came to what they regarded as the holy crusade of 1861. Influenced by the utterances of Lincoln in contrast to those of Jefferson Davis (1808–89), the second series of the *Bigelow Papers* of Lowell particularly expressed the pride of a nation ready to sacrifice itself for its noble ideals of abolition. Later, of course, the Union could identify its aspirations with those of world liberation in its emancipation policies.

☞ A 37.

Strictly speaking, this is a false statement. The president had not dismissed the general, but relayed the message to Army General Omar Bradley (1893–1981), who signed the order of discharge. Even before the order reached MacArthur, he had learned from radio reports that chairman of the Joint Chiefs of Staff Bradley had dismissed him.

☞ A 38.

If one accepts the words of the North Vietnamese General Giap, it was President Ford's decision that the U.S. forces close down the entire American operation in Cambodia when Lon Nol had stepped down in Phnom Penh and a replacement government lacked the strength to materialize. That triggered the final unraveling of the whole South Vietnamese situation. On April 12, 1975, the United States withdrew from Cambodia and had nowhere to go. In his memoirs, General Giap maintained that his forces planned on seizing Saigon in about two years. However, with the American forces in as much disarray as the South Vietnamese, he had to immediately improvise an offensive and this contributed to the resignation of President Nguyen Van Thieu on April 21. The capture of the South Vietnamese capital by Giap on April 28 followed. The war was over.

ANSWERS

☞ A 39.

On April 11, 1814, Napoleon was forced to abdicate. Even though his opponents were defeated several times, they were supplied constantly with new manpower, which Napoleon was not, so his enemies advanced deeply into France. The result of it all was Napoleon's famous exile to Elba.

☞ A 40.

Leary's wife remarried, and her grandson was Langston Hughes (1902–67).

☞ A 41.

Elizabeth didn't want to be associated with the blood-thirstiness of her Tudor ancestors. Besides, Mary was her closest relative and a sovereign princess, which in turn might boomerang and set a precedent against her own personage. After another scheme of deceit to unseat Elizabeth I was scotched, Mary was ready to abdicate her right to the throne and devote herself exclusively to the kingdom of God. Her correspondence in late 1585 from the Castle of Chartley, however, was intercepted and deciphered. The alleged plan was for Anthony Babington to murder Elizabeth, and after a Spanish invasion of England by the prince of Parma, Mary was to be crowned. Mary declared her innocence at Fotheringhay Castle, asking for proof of this scheme in her own handwriting; she felt she was a martyr of her religion and walked cheerfully to her death by beheading (1587).

☞ **A 42.**

President McKinley announced that he had searched his soul and decided that it was his duty to "civilize and Christianize" the Filipinos.

☞ **A 43.**

The English king who visited his island for only a few weeks (1194) while reigning was Richard I (1157–99), known as Richard the Lion-Hearted.

☞ **A 44.**

Virtually nobody on campus listened to the president's speech. The campus, in fact, had erupted into a battle-field, with gunfire, violence, and fires raging out of control everywhere. Countless people were injured, among them dozens of U.S. marshals and students, and a French journalist and a university laborer were killed. Mississippi governor Ross Barnett would not yield and admit Mr. Meredith (b. 1933) and kept arguing with the president on the telephone, so that Mr. Kennedy finally was compelled to call in the U.S. Army to restore order and have Mr. Meredith enrolled.

☞ **A 45.**

General Erich Ludendorff (1865–1937).

☞ **A 46.**

President Franklin D. Roosevelt ordered the assassination of the man who masterminded the attack on Pearl

Harbor, Admiral Isoroku Yamamoto. Shortly after the Japanese admiral's defeat at the decisive naval battle of Midway (1942), which marked the turning point in the Pacific war, he was shot down by U.S. Army P-38s in an air ambush over the Shortland Islands on April 18, 1943, and killed.

☞ **A 47.**

Winnie Mandela (b. 1934).

☞ **A 48.**

The grandsons were Great Britain's George V (1865–1936) and Germany's Kaiser Wilhelm II (1859–1941). Their famous grandmother was Queen Victoria (1819–1901).

☞ **A 49.**

The leader, Sir Roger Casement, landed on the Irish coast, having been taken there by a German U-boat on April 20, 1916. Within four days he and Patrick H. Pearse had organized what is now known as the Easter Rebellion. The insurrection was suppressed in a week largely as a result of the Germans' not coming through with their promised aid. On August 3, Sir Roger and others were hanged after a brief trial.

☞ **A 50.**

The two words the aborigines said to Captain Cook and, eighteen years later, to the white convicts who were ferried over from Europe to colonize Australia, were: *"Warra, warra!"* They mean "Go away!"

☞ A 51.

According to Polk's secretary of the navy, George Bancroft, the following were his four objectives: 1) Removal of tariff restrictions. 2) Establishment of an independent treasury system as well as a Department of the Interior and a U.S. Naval Academy. 3) Peaceful settlement of the Oregon question with Great Britain. 4) Acquisition of California. All four objects were attained in the four years he served in office. Three months later he was dead.

☞ A 52.

The Japanese empire trained hundreds of men to operate the human torpedoes against the Allied fleets. The overall effect of the damage they inflicted was negligible because midget submarines were limited by their small engines and could maneuver only very slowly under water. At the end of the war (September 1945), the Japanese submarine service was down to four boats.

☞ A 53.

Delegates heeded Washington's call and assembled in Philadelphia on May 25, 1787, to debate points to strengthen the charter. Less than four months later, they emerged from Independence Hall with a reinforced draft of a new Constitution for the United States of America.

ANSWERS

☞ A 54.

When Napoleon expelled João VI from Portugal in 1808, the prince regent moved the court to Brazil and the country flourished under his reign. After Napoleon's fall, João VI, now king, raised the former Portuguese colony to the status of a separate kingdom. When the king returned to Portugal in 1821, he named his son, Dom Pedro, regent of Brazil. However, when ordered to return to Portugal, Dom Pedro refused, declared the independence of Brazil, and had himself crowned emperor of Brazil. In 1831, Dom Pedro abdicated in favor of his son Dom Pedro II, who reigned for about fifty years, until he went into exile in 1889 after freeing the slaves. Two years later Brazil was declared a republic.

☞ A 55.

The Russians withdrew under General Stolietov in 1877 and in 1878 the two countries signed a treaty of mutual support. Five years earlier, Moscow had recognized Afghanistan to be within Britain's sphere of influence, and Bukhara (Uzbek) within Russia's. Despite Russia's withdrawal from Kabul, capital of Afghanistan, the British invaded the country and by 1879 the British had gained control of the Kurram Valley, the Khyber Pass, and of Afghan foreign policy. This was only the beginning of the Second Afghan War in the nineteenth century. The occupation of Afghanistan by Soviet forces in the 1980s was nothing new to these mountain people. Only the cast of the occupation army was different.

GENERAL HISTORY

☞ **A 56.**

The fourth belly of the cow is the English translation for the Zulu Isandhlwana. It was on January 22, 1879, that the British Army suffered probably its worst defeat in a hundred years and it took place in Isandhlwana in Natal, South Africa. The British invading force lost 52 officers and 1,277 enlisted men in a single day there and the Zulus, fighting mostly with spears and cowhide shields, were the victors. The Battle of Isandhlwana has been likened to the massacre of George Armstrong Custer (1839–76) and his cavalrymen by the Sioux at the Little Big Horn River three years earlier.

☞ **A 57.**

It was Tolstoy's post-1880 writings, which are known as Tolstoyism. Tolstoy not only advocated Christian love but ordered his followers to abstain from work ordered by the state. His disciples were banished to Siberia for following the dictates of his new creed. At the same time, Tolstoy was excommunicated from the Orthodox Christian church in Russia for renouncing modern Christianity and its rituals and prejudices.

☞ **A 58.**

United States prisoners of war dying at the hands of the Nazis amounted to 1 percent (although many of the POWs were routinely tortured). In Vietnamese hands, death came to about 15 percent of the POWs.

ANSWERS

Thirty-nine percent of American POWs at the mercy of the Japanese or North Korean enemy met death.

☞ A 59.

In the fall of Bataan in April 1942, about ten thousand American soldiers surrendered to the Japanese. The mass surrender came as a complete surprise to the Japanese. The consequence was the notorious Bataan Death March. By the end of the war, more than a third of the American POWs either had died of disease or starvation or were brutally murdered by the Japanese, who simply were not equipped to handle such a huge mass of prisoners.

☞ A 60.

Not quite true. The Belgians never ruled Odessa, but the French did. After the German army ejected the Soviets from Kiev in February 1918, the Ukrainians declared their independence from the Soviet Union for the second time since January 28, 1918, under General Paul Skoropadsky. He was overthrown by Ukrainian Socialists in November 1918, then the French immediately occupied Odessa in December 1918. In April 1919, the Bolsheviks expelled the Allied forces from Odessa (and Kiev) and finally declared the Ukraine a Soviet Republic. In December 1991 Ukraine became independent again.

☞ A 61.

The lady's name was Eleanor of Aquitaine (1122–1204). In 1137, she married a prince who became Louis VII of France. When she bore him two daughters but no sons, the marriage was annulled in 1151. She then married Henry of Anjou, who acceded to the British throne in 1154. The consequences: From that date, strife and wars through the eighteenth century raged between the two countries. Eleanor bore Henry II eight children, five of them sons. She arranged a marriage between one of her granddaughters from her second marriage to one of the grandsons of her first husband. Being an heiress to Aquitaine, she was responsible for uniting that French territory with England for the next four hundred years.

☞ A 62.

On December 9, 1935, students in Beijing protested on the campus of Yenching University, demonstrating against Japanese expansion. With the Japanese far away in their puppet state of Manchuria, the students could utilize their freedom and demonstrate, under Chiang Kai-shek's government, for nationalism and freedom, of which the Japanese were threatening to deprive them. Half a century later, on December 9, 1986, the young rebels once more showed their disapproval, this time of their own autocratic (Communist) government. And almost three years after that event, in June 1989, the whole world watched the televised prodemocracy demonstrations by Chinese students in Tiananmen Square in Beijing before they were crushed by government forces.

☞ A 63.

The philosopher was David Hume (1711–76), whose emphasis on civic virtue influenced the Founding Fathers in their framing of the Constitution. Hume himself based this segment of his philosophy on the writings and speeches of Cicero (106–43 B.C.).

☞ A 64.

Patrols of the 273rd regiment, 69th division, 5th corps of the U.S. First Army met Soviet patrols in the vicinity of Torgau on the River Elbe on that fateful day, April 25, 1945. It was the first time the eastern and western allies joined hands in the European theater of war and became a symbol of the United Nations Charter that was being drafted that day thousands of miles away in San Francisco.

☞ A 65.

When Dracula's father, Vlad Dracul, prince of Wallachia, was replaced on the Wallachian throne in 1443, he was forced into a close agreement with Sultan Mehmed II. To secure his alliance the Turkish sultan demanded two of Dracul's sons as hostages: Radu and Dracula. They grew up in an atmosphere of brutality and violence. Dracula escaped and led Wallachian forces against the Ottomans without, however, killing the sultan. After many battles Dracula was defeated and the king of Hungary put him in the prison of Buda where Dracula, now desperate, practiced the brutalities he had learned at the sultan's court. King Mattjias put him under house arrest, hoping to use his brutal talents against the Turks, and later authorized him to wage his war of terror. Although Dracula captured Bucharest, becoming prince of Wallachia again, the boyars, the privileged class of Romania, never forgetting Dracula's reign of terror, assassinated him. When the Turks later surged across the Danube, the Romanians saw Dracula as a defender of Christianity against the Ottoman Empire, and made him a national hero.

☞ A 66.

Andrew Jackson wrote it in 1828 when he campaigned for the presidency against John Quincy Adams, whose Adams-Clay press set had accused Jackson of adultery. Jackson refused to be drawn into the trap of unleashing an attack on Adams's wife.

☞ A 67.

The statesman was Count Camillo Benso di Cavour (1810–61). The state was Piedmont in Northern Italy. With Garibaldi's (1807–82) aid, he helped to unify most of Italy in 1861 after many battles and insurrections, and died three months later, at age fifty-one.

☞ A 68.

There was one overriding reason for the delay in ratifying the Articles of Confederation: land-grabbing. Virginia claimed all of the West north of her southern border and west of Maryland. The Indiana Company tried to persuade Philadelphia to insist on Virginia's ceding her western land claims to the Confederation. Benjamin Franklin wrote a tract attacking this land-grabbing business, as did Thomas Paine with his *The Public Good*. Congress passed a resolution on October 10, 1780, that promised any western land ceded to the United States would be settled into clearly marked republican states so they could become members of the Federal Union. Maryland was the last holdout; it finally ratified the Articles in March 1781 because its assembly saw it was futile to go on playing the speculator's game all by itself.

☞ **A 69.**

The French diplomat Ferdinand de Lesseps (1805–94) made his name by becoming the builder of the Suez Canal. On May 29, 1849, the French government sent him to the Roman Republic to sign a treaty that stipulated that the city's gates be opened to the French army in return for a promise by the French to respect the rights of the Roman Republic and to protect it against foreign aggression. Fate, however, determined that a French election led to a change in foreign policy and de Lesseps was abruptly recalled to Paris and disavowed. Disillusioned, de Lesseps accepted an invitation from his friend, Said Pasha, now viceroy of Egypt, who on November 30, 1854, granted him a concession and the money to pierce the isthmus of the Suez with a canal, which he completed in 1869. He was also commissioned by the French in 1879 to build the Panama Canal, but after eight years he failed and was obliged to give up the project.

☞ **A 70.**

Ironically, it was his firmness. In his own words: "It has ever been a certain position with me that firmness is the characteristic of an Englishman." And "I know I'm doing my duty and, therefore, can never wish to retract." He flatly refused to make any political concessions to anybody. Nevertheless, the English people, to a large extent, supported his American policies. Ten years before he died, in 1820, he had to be restrained in a straitjacket because he had become violently insane.

☞ **A 71.**

Their promise proved to be a lie. Over the next sixteen years, the French government had to pay enormous ransom amounts for the release of some thousand French prisoners, which the Vietnamese Communists were still holding.

☞ **A 72.**

James Polk (1795–1849) served for one term (1845–49). He did not seek the presidency but was only a compromise candidate. Completely exhausted by the efforts he had expended in the White House, Polk died three months after serving as president.

☞ **A 73.**

In 1961 Charlayne Hunter, at the age of nineteen, was the first African-American student (with Hamilton Holmes) at the University of Georgia in 175 years. She was subjected to a campaign of vilification and mobs of hostile students, except for Marcia Powell and the man who later became the publisher of the *Los Angeles Times,* Tom Johnson. Ms. Hunter received her degree in journalism in June 1963. Although she was never treated with quite as much hostility as in her first forty-eight hours on campus, when riots broke out outside the Center Myers dormitory where she lived, her stay at the university was never normal. Later to become

ANSWERS

Charlayne Hunter-Gault, the black woman made her name as a *New York Times* correspondent and as the national news anchor and field reporter for TV's "Mac-Neil/Lehrer Newshour."

☞ **A 74.**

Uncle Sam's figure was first drawn by Thomas Nast (1840–1902) in the late nineteenth century. Nast also originated the Democratic party's donkey, the Republican party's elephant, and Tammany's tiger. Uncle Sam is not an abbreviation for the United States of America. There was a man by the name of Samuel Wilson who in the early part of the nineteenth century was a contractor of the U.S. government for preserved beef. The beef was delivered to army posts and elsewhere in big barrels and boxes marked "U.S." Soldiers referred to these boxes as coming from Uncle Sam.

☞ **A 75.**

The lieutenant governor wrote: "I do not scruple to pronounce that in the whole world there is not a worse country."

☞ **A 76.**

In 1776, the ragged army was Washington's. He evacuated his army across the East River to Manhattan when British General Howe failed to do so from his stronghold in Staten Island. From there Washington withdrew to White Plains and New Jersey. Hounded by Cornwallis, Washington won a battle at Trenton and, after crossing the Delaware River at night on December 26, 1776, at Princeton. Howe would not join British General Burgoyne after these two defeats, leaving Burgoyne to fight the battles of Saratoga largely on his own. He attacked the American army commanded by the timid General Gates on Bemis's Heights (September 19, 1777), but one brave American general inflicted heavy losses on Burgoyne at Freeman's Farm, and on October 7, the same brave American general inflicted a severe defeat on the British army. Some of the British withdrew into Canada; France and Spain became allies of the United States. The name of the brave American general: Benedict Arnold (1741–1801). Feeling slighted that his deeds were not appreciated by the Americans and after being reprimanded by Washington for two trivial offenses, Arnold thought traitorously he would be better appreciated by the British.

☞ **A 77.**

It did not help to abolish slavery. In order to obtain the support of the South, the Convention delegates agreed to count a slave as "three-fifths of a free man" as a base for electing representatives and paying taxes. There were no restrictions on the importing of slaves for twenty years. The reason for all this, however, was not altogether racist. It was the price the country had to pay for the support of Southern delegates in the new centralized federal government. Without this endorsement, the central government would not have been united and powerful enough to destroy the evil of slavery in the future.

ANSWERS

☞ A 78.

What the two ships have in common is that they are both fictional. In 1898, fourteen years before the *Titanic* sank, Morgan Robinson penned a novella entitled *Futility*. A short time later it was republished as *The Wreck of the Titan*. Virtually everything described in the 1898 novel closely parallels the sinking of the *Titanic*. A couple of differences, though: The *Titanic* did not run up an iceberg but brushed by it and was only doing 22.5 knots at the time of the collision. The second ship comes from W. T. Stead's novel *From the Old West to the New*, which came out in December 1892. The coincidence here is not only that the captain of the liner *Majestic* in the novel is E. J. Smith, but that this was also the name of the real-life captain of the *Titanic*. Another irony is that the fictional *Majestic* came to the rescue of a liner that had struck an iceberg and sunk. A more tragic irony is that the author, W. T. Stead, booked passage on the *Titanic* and went down with it.

☞ A 79.

To 25 million persons. It must be pointed out, however, that not all 19 million people were killed by the Japanese. Others fled or died of disease, starvation, and in battles between Mao's guerrillas and Chiang Kai-shek's nationalist armies.

☞ A 80.

No, not Imelda Marcos. She did not spend $2,700,000 on a single pair of earrings. The woman in question was

Marie Antoinette (1755–93). The populace indeed threw her out, then had her guillotined in Paris in the Place de la Concorde in October 1793, although for other faults besides her extravagance. She never grasped how the flaunting of her wealth and privilege could have antagonized the poverty-stricken people of France.

☞ **A 81.**

Abraham Lincoln, in 1860.

☞ **A 82.**

Hitler's brownshirts were not the first. The earliest storm troopers were a German infantry regiment specially equipped with gas masks and 7.9-mm carbine rifles with bayonets. These storm troopers were fighting around the French Champagne region in the spring of 1918.

☞ **A 83.**

His name was Philander Knox (1853–1921), and he was the attorney general of the United States. The occasion for this statement: When President Theodore Roosevelt (1858–1919) encouraged an insurrection in the Colombian province of Panama so that he could intervene and build a canal through it.

☞ **A 84.**

President François Mitterrand (b. 1916) of France.

ANSWERS

☞ A 85.

True. He suspended the right of habeas corpus and arrested many citizens just because they were Democrats. He also imposed martial law in 1861. The Constitution gives this power to Congress only, but Lincoln took the power upon himself and refused to recall Congress in session to debate the question.

☞ A 86.

The first attempt to sail from Southampton, England, on August 5, 1620, was unsuccessful, but of the 103 passengers leaving Plymouth, England, on September 6, 103 arrived in what is today Massachusetts. However, they were not the same 103 passengers. Two of them had died on the voyage across the Atlantic, and two new passengers were born on board. The choice to land in Plymouth, Massachusetts, was determined by the ship's prematurely exhausted supply of beer. One of the passenger's manuscripts from 1622 records: "For we could not now take time for further search or consideration; our victuals being much spent, especially our beer. . . ."

☞ A 87.

Thomas Jefferson wrote the words to John Adams's wife in Paris on hearing about the bloody riots in Massachusetts in 1786 and 1787.

☞ A 88.

In the Eastern-bloc countries. Most of the armaments sent by the United States to the anti-Communist insurgents were AK-47 automatic rifles built in Poland. Eastern-bloc nations also supplied the anti-Sandinistas via Israel and Honduras with RPG-7 rocket launchers.

☞ A 89.

Because Captain Todd was not engaged at the time in a Civil War battle. He helped to accost and almost destroy the infamous Quantrill gang with his group of Union soldiers. The Quantrill gang of 450 men had terrorized Lawrence, Kansas, just a few weeks earlier, killing 140 of its citizens and robbing them and their families. Captain Todd not only broke up the gang but killed one of the arch-murderers and loyal lieutenants of William Clarke Quantrill: his own namesake, George Todd.

☞ A 90.

Thus far in the twentieth century, Ms. Bhutto is the only head of government to give birth (January 25, 1990) while in office.

☞ A 91.

The Battle of Verdun in World War I in February 1916. French Chief of Staff Joffre removed most of the guns around Verdun, having lost all faith in forts, and used them in preparation of the summer Somme offensive. After four months, on July 11, the Germans took Verdun, inflicting heavy losses on the French, about 400,000 men. The French now had to reduce their military manpower, leaving most of the fighting to the British. The Germans withdrew many divisions from the eastern front as a rescue operation for their own heavily suffering troops. There was no clear-cut victory for either side since neither adversary attained its objectives. Verdun had little strategic value to either side; it was a hard-to-defend location with poor communications, and Joffre (1852–1931) was more interested in the Somme area, where the British and French could collaborate more easily. About five million men fought in the Battle of Verdun. The French defended Verdun more for patriotic reasons associated with the town than for its limited strategic value.

☞ A 92.

Of course, politics was involved, as when Stalin filled the Congress with his own cronies and delegates outside Moscow and Petrograd. But there was personal animosity as well. The mortally ill Lenin was enraged by Stalin heaping abuse on Lenin's wife, Nadezhda Krupskaya (1869–1939). In fact, on March 5, 1923, when Lenin was already paralyzed from his second stroke, he dictated a letter to Stalin in which he threatened that unless Stalin apologized to Krupskaya because of his rudeness to her, he would break all relations with him. Stalin waited until Lenin's health had sunk to a level where his half-hearted apology was hardly comprehended by Lenin, who no longer had the strength to act rationally one way or the other.

☞ A 93.

Muslims and Hindus were members of an Indian organization devoted exclusively to plundering, murdering, and burying their victims. In Sanskrit, the word *conceal* is *sthag*, and the organization was called *Thags* or *Thugs*.

Hundreds of the Thugs were captured by Indian-British authorities and hanged. Their fraternity was as good as extinct in the early 1850s. The word *thugs,* however, still exists and implies today what it did 150 years ago in India.

☞ A 94.

Frederick the Great of Prussia played host to French philosopher, dramatist, satirist, and historian Voltaire (1694–1778) from 1751 to 1753. They conversed only in French, which the Prussian king spoke more fluently than his native German. Intellectually stimulating, the visit was frequently on the verge of collapse due to Voltaire's forgeries, disputes with the royal court in Potsdam, and his being placed under house arrest. However, many dramatic reconciliations prolonged the visit to almost two years.

☞ A 95.

The workers were dissatisfied because of the absence of any radical program and by the small success of the February 1917 uprising. Lenin presented a clean break with the oppressive past as well as an attitude toward society—and especially the war—that found powerful echoes among the workers. Thousands of them awaited Lenin enthusiastically on his return from exile abroad, having the day off from work as the result of a Russian Orthodox holiday.

☞ A 96.

The conversation really did take place. However, these words, taken from his diary, were uttered by General de

ANSWERS

Caulaincourt when he addressed Napoleon in October 1812, while both of them were already in Moscow. By that time the Russians had burned Moscow, frustrating Napoleon's hope to bring Czar Alexander I (1777–1825) to terms. A few days after the conversation with his general, Napoleon realized the futility of maintaining his troops so far from his bases and he began his disastrous retreat from Moscow.

☞ A 97.

The czar took command of his armies because the Germans and Austrians had defeated Russia on every front. The Russians had lost all of Poland, Lithuania, and Courland, a province of Latvia, all the way from Riga to Pinsk and south to Dubno, Tarnopol, and Czernowitz. His throne was endangered. The Battle of Lake Naroch (March 19–April 30, 1916) was supposed to put the pressure on the Germans at Verdun, but the Russian offensive was so inconclusive that it had no effect benefiting the French.

☞ A 98.

Because Cesare's father, Pope Alexander VI, had just asked Urbino's kind, honest ruler, Guidobaldo I, to lend the papal army Urbino's artillery. This was done, and Cesare Borgia immediately attacked and conquered with it the undefended city of Urbino on June 21, 1502. As usual, he treated the conquered inhabitants with gentleness, but he seized and sold Guidobaldo's art collection in order to pay his army, which had a retinue of poets and prostitutes to keep the soldiers content.

GENERAL HISTORY

☞ A 99.

Although the Russians advanced 125 kilometers and took half a million German prisoners, the Kaiser threw fifteen new German divisions from the west into the eastern battles (to the detriment of the German forces on the Somme); the Russians once more fell back, missing their primary objectives of Lemberg and Kovel. Their own losses now amounted to a million men, leaving the Russian army more demoralized than ever and serving as a prelude to the Treaty of Brest-Litovsk (March 3, 1918), which Germany forced upon Lenin's Soviets, but which the defeated Germany had to renounce in 1919.

☞ A 100.

The man was the Marquis de Lafayette (1757–1834). He led several victorious battles on George Washington's side and later became the first commander of the National Guard in Paris and a champion of the National Assembly. Just about the time Tom Paine became a member of the National Assembly in 1792, the latter declared Lafayette a traitor for favoring a limited monarchy. Lafayette escaped to Austria, where he was jailed and, with Napoleon's help, released in 1797. Even though Napoleon considered him a simpleton, he respected Lafayette and placed him on the retired army list. About twenty-five years later he became a liberal member of France's Chamber of Deputies and returned for a fifteen-month tour of the United States, where he received the adulation of the American people and their leaders, who named a city in Indiana after him.

ANSWERS

☞ A 101.

The woman was Marie Bonaparte, the last surviving member of the Bonaparte family to carry that name. She lived from 1882 to 1962 and was the daughter of the emperor's great-nephew.

☞ A 102.

Jefferson's lover was Sally Hemings, a black woman. But she was much more than a slave, much closer to him than is generally believed. Her father was John Wayles, the father of Jefferson's wife. Jefferson had married the young widow, Martha Wayles Skelton, in January 1772. Sally Hemings's mother, Elizabeth, who was half-white, was by law still a slave, and she had to pass the bondage on to her children by Wayles. Sally Hemings accompanied Marie (Polly) Jefferson, Jefferson's daughter, to Paris in the spring of 1787. There the two lived for more than two years and studied French and music. In London she met Abigail Adams.

☞ A 103.

President Reagan hugely increased the firepower of the RDF both in the Persian Gulf for the army and air force and in the Pacific for the navy. However, it was the Carter administration that first created and developed the RDF. What actually helped to accelerate the development of the largely dormant American military emergency force was the increasingly large force being deployed by the Soviet Union on the Iranian frontier.

☞ A 104.

In the Seven Years' War (1756–63), England and Prussia, after victories at Rossbach and Leuthen, suffered a crushing defeat in Kunersdorf from which they were only saved by Russia's withdrawal and, later, its 1762 peace offer. One of the results of the Peace Treaty of Paris in 1763 was that Spain surrendered Florida to Great Britain. More important, England and Prussia defeated France, Austria, Russia, Sweden, and Saxony. The war originated over boundary disputes in North America and was carried on by land in America and Germany and by sea in all parts of the world.

☞ A 105.

The rebel was an impoverished farmer and former captain in the Continental Army of the United States named Daniel Shays (1747–1825). Historians would remember the disturbance in Massachusetts in 1786 and 1787 as "Shays' Rebellion." He was reluctant to use arms against the courts to avoid bloodshed. Only when the taxes on the destitute farmers were increased in 1786 did the rebels seek recourse through the use of arms. On February 4, 1787, the rebel army, "The Regulators," was defeated in Petersham. Eight of the men were hanged, many imprisoned, while Shays and others escaped to New York. In spite of a pardon, Shays refused to return to Massachusetts and died, forgotten, in 1825.

☞ A 106.

No. There is no mention in any April 1917 records of Stalin being present on this occasion. It was Stalin himself who commissioned painters to invent this scene. He waited until several years later, after Lenin had died and could not contradict him.

☞ A 107.

Britain suffered economically because with the onset of the American Civil War, all American cotton supplies for the hundreds of English textile mills were cut off, causing widespread unemployment and economic hardship in the British Isles.

☞ A 108.

Queen Mary, indeed, was responsible for the slaughter of English Protestants, but not the devout Catholic Mary Queen of Scots, better known as Mary Stuart. Mary I, also called Mary Tudor, was the culprit. She was the daughter of Catherine of Aragon and Henry VIII, and she became queen in 1553. For the next five years, she repealed all Protestant laws, England became a nominally Catholic country again, and three hundred Protestants were burned at the stake for heresy. Mary became known as "Bloody Mary." After she died, in 1558, her half-sister, Queen Elizabeth I, repealed all the Catholic laws.

☞ A 109.

The last prisoner in the Tower of London was Hitler's deputy, Rudolf Hess (1894–1987). After he parachuted near Glasgow, Scotland, in 1940, he was imprisoned in the Tower of London during World War II.

GENERAL HISTORY

☞ A 110.

The Bill of Rights is partially based on a document that greatly influenced the American Constitution—the British Bill of Rights, which was drawn up by Parliament in 1689. It was assented to by William of Orange as a condition for his becoming king of Great Britain, with Mary II of the Netherlands becoming queen. This Bill of Rights guaranteed Englishmen liberties such as the right to petition and habeas corpus, which could not be taken away by the king.

☞ A 111.

More than six million troops faced each other in Europe in August 1914. To avenge the disgrace of 1870, the French were eager to march on Berlin under General Foch. The German Kaiser (Wilhelm II) wanted to knock out France with his Chief of Staff von Moltke, using the German Schlieffen Plan. The Austro-Hungarian Empire was intent on defeating the Serbs and Russians under von Hötzendorf by declaring war on Serbia on July 28, 1914. The Russians under Grand Duke Nicholas and the French under General Joffre were determined to attack the rest of Germany with Britain and defeat it. All general staffs lay under the spell of Clausewitz, and within two weeks of the pronouncement of general mobilization in August 1914, the largest collision of armies were battling each other on the western and eastern fronts and in the Balkans.

☞ A 112.

In spite of several attempts the three Roman emperors could not invade Scotland because Pictish tribes constantly raided Roman England. Hadrian finally ordered the construction of a seventy-three-mile-long wall from Solway Firth to the Tyne (completed in A.D. 128) to keep out the invaders from the north. England was the only country the Romans invaded in which they left little imprint, except for some fortifications, baths, and the language.

☞ A 113.

Two years after the Jewish rebel leader Bar Kochba expelled the Romans from Jerusalem (A.D. 132), the despotic Roman Emperor Hadrian (A.D. 76–138) seized it again, destroyed it completely, and named it Aelia Capitolina. It became little more than a Roman military camp. Hadrian succeeded in eliminating many Jewish communities. Some of these fled to England and, ironically, settled not far from Hadrian's Wall. Had Hadrian lived for much longer than two years after the Jewish rebellion ended, he would have been successful in destroying Palestinian Jewry completely. His successors were much more lenient toward the remaining Jews.

☞ A 114.

Gandhi received written assurances from South Africa's Colonial Secretary Jan Smuts (1870–1950) that a law regarding Asiatics would be enforced in a just manner and with due regard to vested interests. Feeling that he had achieved as much as could be guaranteed at the time, Gandhi returned to India while Smuts was involved in the colonial war against German Southwest Africa.

☞ A 115.

Weizmann (1874–1952) was a brilliant scientist who discovered a means to synthesize acetone, which was basic to British munitions production in World War I. Weizmann declined any financial reward from the British government, especially from Lloyd George (1863–1945), who was minister of munitions in 1915. Weizmann's wish was to help the British war effort, hoping that this gesture of generosity would help the cause of the Jewish people. It did. He was largely responsible for winning from the British government in 1917 the famous Balfour Declaration. Later he became cofounder and head of state of Israel.

☞ A 116.

The journalist Ernie Pyle said, "Any G.I. who didn't have at least two girls on his arms was an exhibitionist."

☞ A 117.

Her order was not carried out because her own *Hofjuden* (court Jews) interceded with several European sovereigns who had been seeking fiscal aid as they competed for wealth, prestige, and power. These princes in turn successfully interceded with Maria Theresa, who then rescinded her edict.

☞ A 118.

The name of the American captain was Abraham Lincoln. The war later became known as the Black Hawk War of 1832.

ANSWERS

☞ A 119.

The last country to declare war on Germany in World War I was Honduras, on July 19, 1918, just over three months before the armistice.

☞ A 120.

True. Catholics and Jews were not permitted in those institutions. Today, however, there is no religious or racial discrimination regarding these matters.

☞ A 121.

It was the excuse used for starting the war. But the Austro-Hungarian Empire had long wanted to attack Serbia and Russia. For four weeks the German government urged Austria to resume Austro-Russian negotiations. Despite numerous German warnings, Russia decided for general mobilization. Within a few days in August 1914, Germany declared war on Russia and France, Britain declared war on Germany, and Austria declared war on Serbia and Russia. World War I had started.

☞ A 122.

The first known invasion took place in the Middle East, when Asia Minor fell to the Hittites after 2000 B.C. The first battle of which there is an *established* record was fought in Megiddo in 1479 B.C., when the Egyptians attempted to reconquer Palestine under the command of Thutmose III. He defeated the Hyksos leader, the King of Kadesh, and his tribe, sometimes referred to as the "Shepherd Kings," and he was involved in earlier chariot battles. The tribe also invaded Egypt in 1680 B.C., but little is known of these battles.

☞ A 123.

True. Postwar is correct, too. But not post–World War II. The Danes (Vikings) invaded England in 871, but King Alfred the Great (c. 848–c. 900) checked the Danish advance on the battlefield of Edington in 878. The Danes, however, continued to attack English counties north of London. That is when the English collected a special tax from their own people, which they called *Danegeld,* to bribe the Danes and to build an army to defend London successfully when the Danish king, Sweyn I Forkbeard (ruled 985–1014), attacked the capital in 994. The Danes still ruled England under King Canute (c. 995–1035) and his sons until 1042 when Edward the Confessor (c. 1003–66) finally became king of England.

☞ A 124.

The name of the British politician was Henry John Temple, Third Viscount Palmerston (1784–1865). His attitude toward the Civil War was officially neutral, but his sympathies were with the South.

☞ A 125.

The other maritime disaster happened in the Gulf of St. Lawrence. The ship that went down in 1914 was the *Empress of Ireland.* Over a thousand passengers and crew drowned in that disaster, which occurred in a fog when this Canadian Pacific ship collided with a Norwegian collier. It resulted in the most fatalities of any maritime collision in the twentieth century, yet few people alive today have heard of it.

☞ A 126.

The first mourning stamps of that nature appeared in 1945 in memory of President Franklin Delano Roosevelt. These memorial stamps were issued in Haiti, Hungary, Greece, Honduras, and Nicaragua shortly after the U.S. president's death. Later such stamps were also issued in Brazil, Guatemala, and El Salvador.

☞ A 127.

The disinterred corpse was Oliver Cromwell's. He had King Charles I (1600–49) beheaded and thought he had abolished the monarchy forever. Three years after Cromwell's death in 1658, Charles's son, the new king, Charles II (1630–85), avenged his father by vilifying Cromwell's corpse.

☞ A 128.

The British did try. In fact, the first British high commissioner, Sir Herbert Samuels, himself a Jew, leaned over backward trying to accommodate Arab interests. He even convened a General Arab Council, hoping to facilitate cooperation between Jews and Arabs. The Arabs wanted no part of it. The proposal to partition Palestine into a Jewish and Arab state, recommended by Lord Peel's Royal Commission, was rejected by Jews and Arabs alike. At the beginning of World War II, after years of this political stalemate, England feared for its imports of oil from the Middle East and began to limit Jewish immigration to Palestine.

☞ A 129.

Napoleon defeated the Allied armies, which were stretched almost from Nice to Genoa. He beat Baron Colli's Piedmontese army at Mondovi (April 21, 1796), then turned on Beaulieu's Austrian rear guard at Lodi (May 10, 1796), personally leading a bayonet charge across the town's bridge. This above all endeared the young general to his men and shut him in their hearts for as long as he ruled.

☞ A 130.

For almost the same reason that Sir Winston Churchill considered World War II in his great multi-volume series *The Second World War* one single war, even though military battles raged at different times in various parts of the world with long lulls of peace (the Phony Peace) in between, from 1939 to 1945. While Churchill had the opportunity to complete this literary series and other historical works, Thucydides could complete the Archidamian War books only, constantly redefining various stages in his work, supplemented by fresh inquiries, while the second part of *The History of the Peloponnesian War* (the Ionian War), with the temporary Peace of Nicias in 421 B.C., stops in the middle of the political and military upheavals during the fall of 411 B.C., with seven more years of the war completely unrecorded by him. Thucydides considered these battles part of a sin-

ANSWERS

gle war since they had the same objective: a Spartan defeat at the hands of the Athenians. Plainly, Thucydides was deeply hurt by the fact that he was banned from Athens for twenty years when he failed to prevent the seizure of Amphipolis by the Spartan Brasidas. During his twenty-year refuge abroad he started to write *The History of the Peloponnesian War* with an objectivity that has rarely been equaled. Book Four, for instance, describes his own defeat as an Athenian general at the hands of the Spartans. However, the historical record ends abruptly after Book Eight, well before Thucydides could describe Athens' capitulation in 404 B.C. to Sparta. Thucydides was murdered in 400 B.C. before he could finish the history.

☞ A 131.

At first Congress started out in Princeton, New Jersey, in June 1783, then shifted to Annapolis, Maryland, five months later, then moved to Trenton, New Jersey, in 1784, and a year later to New York City, where it stayed until the Confederation ended in 1790. At that time New York became the temporary federal capital (1789–90).

☞ A 132.

His name was John Dickinson (1732–1808). He served for the states of Delaware and Pennsylvania because these two states had the same proprietor and the same governor. He was sent from Pennsylvania to the Stamp Act Congress in 1765 and in 1786 represented Delaware at the Annapolis Convention; in 1787 he worked for the same state at the Federal Constitutional Convention. Dickinson was known as the "penman of the Revolution."

☞ **A 133.**

Arthur was later known as the Duke of Wellington.

☞ **A 134.**

The pessimistic observation was made by John Adams (1735–1826), who was elected the first vice president of the United States. He had changed his mind by 1797 when he became the second and last Federalist president.

☞ **A 135.**

Britain's Colonial Secretary Joseph Chamberlain (1836–1914) was the man. This Christian's pro-Jewish sense was fired by his long discussion with Theodor Herzl (1860–1904), who found success only in England for his plan to settle the Jews of the world in Palestine. Chamberlain, in turn, persuaded the British cabinet, headed by Arthur James Balfour (1848–1930), to accept Herzl's idea before World War I. His fervor in behalf of Zionism was purely humanitarian, partly based on his repugnance for the East European pogroms and the Dreyfus affair. But he held it also served as a British penetration into the Ottoman-dominated Palestine. In 1917, Balfour was foreign minister under Prime Minister Lloyd George, who favored the Balfour Declaration.

☞ **A 136.**

The writer was Thomas Paine. He rebutted Burke's *Reflections on the Revolution in France.* His work: *Rights*

ANSWERS

of Man. England's Prime Minister Pitt (1759–1806), fearing a bloody revolution at home as a consequence of Paine's work, had the writer indicted for treason, but Paine escaped to France and was elected to the revolutionary French Convention. Since Paine advocated exile rather than execution of Louis XVI, Robespierre had him imprisoned. After the fall of Robespierre in 1794, however, Paine was readmitted to the Convention and wrote his *Age of Reason.* The British Reform Bill of 1832 can be attributed to the philosophy expounded in Paine's writings.

☞ A 137.

The American who had a liaison with a married woman was Alexander Hamilton. It is assumed that Hamilton was trapped into an affair with Maria Reynolds so that her husband could blackmail him for money. Hamilton, indeed, paid James Reynolds some "silence money," but when Reynolds became more demanding, Hamilton confessed the whole sordid story to President Adams. When the press heard about it in 1797, Hamilton suspected the president of the leak and wrote a pamphlet detailing his affair with Maria Reynolds. It diluted the sensationalism presented by the press, and when Elizabeth Schuyler Hamilton stood firmly by her husband's side throughout the ordeal the American public lost interest in the Reynolds affair, which faded into history.

☞ A 138.

What these items have in common is the date: April 12, 1961. All three events happened on that momentous day.

☞ **A 139.**

Long before the Nazis came to power, the commander of the British forces in South Africa's Boer War (1899–1902), Lord Horatio Kitchener (1850–1916), had these camps built at the turn of the century in South Africa. Here he rounded up his enemies, the native Afrikaners, whose guerrilla units (*kommandos*) attacked the British. Of the 60,000 white settlers taken by Kitchener, approximately 26,000 women and children succumbed to disease and famine in the camps in which they were *concentrated*. One ironical sidelight: After Hitler was poised to invade England in 1940, German refugees (Jews) from Nazi Germany were detained in British camps for part of World War II. One of these camps was called Camp Kitchener.

☞ **A 140.**

The South Africa Act of 1909, which prohibited blacks from sitting in the administrative government building, was not passed in Cape Town but by the British Parliament in London. Moreover, the South African administrative seat of government is not located in Cape Town, but in the administrative capital, Pretoria. The houses of Parliament, however, can be found in Cape Town.

☞ **A 141.**

It is certainly true. During the mud-slinging 1950 campaign for the U.S. Senate, the two California opponents were Richard M. Nixon and Helen Gahagan Douglas, the wife of movie star Melvyn Douglas. Ms. Douglas, oddly enough, started off this notoriously dirty campaign for the Senate seat by charging Nixon was soft on Communism. Mr. Nixon won the election.

☞ A 142.

What the samurai valued above life was honor, unquestioning obedience, and loyalty. The code that stressed these three characteristics was known by the name of *bushido.*

☞ A 143.

Among the many attributes that can be credited to General Washington was one in particular: He was an agriculturist. He wrote in his diary that he had his gardener separate the male from the pistillate (female) flower of the Indian hemp plant. The stalk of the hemp plant contains the fiber for making rope. But the dried leaves and flowering tops of the pistillate hemp plant are the sources of the drug cannabis, better known as marijuana. Whether the general used this end product for smoking or just as an interesting botanical sideline has never been revealed, however.

☞ A 144.

Argentina.

☞ A 145.

The nasty Roman emperor was Gaius, better known as Caligula. His sister Agrippina (the Younger) was accused of poisoning her second husband, Passienus Crispus, in A.D. 49, then married her uncle Claudius and induced him to have his son Britannicus forgo the throne in favor of her own son Nero. In A.D. 54, she is supposed to have poisoned her uncle-husband Claudius, but soon after quarrelled with her son Nero, opposing his liaison with Poppaea. Nero was anything but grateful to his mother for all the trouble she had taken on his behalf and tried to have her drowned on a vessel specially constructed to founder. Agrippina survived, so he simply had her stabbed to death at her country house in A.D. 59.

☞ A 146.

England's Admiral Horatio Nelson (1758–1805) at the Battle of the Nile on August 1, 1798. He destroyed the French fleet in the harbor of Aboukir near Alexandria. Even though Napoleon succeeded in capturing Cairo a short time later, he realized that there was nothing to be done in Egypt and that he and his armies were needed much more urgently in France, where he returned in 1799 to continue the Revolution and prevent a return of the Bourbons. In any case, the British defeated the French in Egypt the following year after Napoleon had left.

☞ A 147.

Rhode Island declined to send delegates to the Constitutional Convention in Philadelphia because its agriculturists were afraid that the new Constitution would deprive the state of its local privileges. In May 1790, Rhode Island ratified the Federal Constitution because the United States passed a bill severing all commercial relations between the United States and Rhode Island.

ANSWERS

☞ A 148.

This occurred in 1793 in France, under War Minister Lazare Carnot (1801–88), when the country was on the verge of collapse due to outside military pressure and the extremes of the French Revolution led to civil war. Within a year, Carnot cleared French soil of foreign occupation troops. By 1795, the French had swept over Holland and made peace with Prussia, Spain, Hanover, and Saxony.

☞ A 149.

The Jacobins of the French Revolution were self-appointed "watchdogs of the revolution"—the Red Guards of the eighteenth century. After a number of French generals suffered military defeats at the hands of the Allies (the British, Dutch, Portuguese, Spanish, Tuscan, and Neapolitan forces), in 1793 the Jacobins beheaded one of those generals—Adam Philippe Custine—on the order of the Committee of Public Safety, established by the national Convention. This body had political commissars spying and interfering on behalf of the committee. All this occurred even before Robespierre commenced "The Terror" in Paris, during which 1,400 royalists, intellectuals, and imagined opponents were executed.

☞ A 150.

The area was Sumer, site of the world's earliest civilization, circa 3800 B.C., located in lower Mesopotamia in what is today part of Iraq. After the third dynasty of Ur was destroyed and the Semitic people from the desert established the dynasties of Isin, Larsa, and Babylon, the Sumerian language as a spoken word slowly disappeared. During the Old Babylonian period Sumerian was used only in cuneiform writing. Some administrative texts were bilingual, in Sumerian and Babylonian (or Akkadian). Old Sumerian literary compositions were put down in writing in Sumerian for the first time during this period although only Babylonian was spoken. By the time of Christ, the Sumerian language had vanished from the face of the earth.

☞ A 151.

Massachusetts became the first state in the Union to allow blacks to serve in the organized militia. The year was 1861.

☞ A 152.

The last Habsburg, reigning from 1916 to 1918, was Charles I of Austria, also known as Charles IV of Hungary. After the fall of the Habsburgs, he went into exile on Madeira where he died in 1922, at age thirty-five. He is buried on the Portuguese island in a church on a hill in the village of Monte.

☞ A 153.

This very plane (one of six built at the same time) took off from Washington in President Wilson's presence, inaugurating American airmail service. It never made Philadelphia. The inexperienced pilot was forced to land in Waldorf, Maryland, twenty miles from the nation's capital, touching down on soil so soft that the plane nosed over and came to rest lying upside down.

ANSWERS

The irony is that, in the best-known error in philately, a number of postage stamps commemorating the festive occasion were printed upside down. One stamp shows airplane number 38262 upside down on the stamp's face. Each of these carmine-and-blue 24-cent 1918 stamps (nicknamed the "Inverted Jenny") is worth in excess of $115,000 today. They were all printed weeks before the unfortunate flight.

☞ A 154.

The first lady was the wife of Abraham Lincoln, Mary Todd Lincoln (1818–82). Since she meddled in matters that were none of her concern, Mrs. Lincoln made many enemies in the White House. In addition, her family connections in the Confederacy aroused serious suspicions about her loyalty, although these proved totally unwarranted. The death of her husband and two of her three children brought on signs of acute mental instability. Her third child, Robert Todd, had her institutionalized for four months in a private sanatorium in 1875, fearing that she would squander her estate and commit suicide. Robert Todd Lincoln served as secretary of war from 1881 to 1885.

☞ A 155.

Simón Bolívar (1783–1830), the Venezuelan general who helped free South America from Spanish rule. All over Latin America, Bolívar is called the "Liberator."

☞ A 156.

The 369th U.S. Infantry was made up of African-Americans.

☞ A 157.

Washington made this observation in a letter to Lafayette. He referred to the American Constitution, which had been signed the day before, on September 17, 1787, in Philadelphia.

☞ A 158.

What was unique was that Michael (b. 1921) ruled Romania *before* his father, Carol II of Romania. Michael was only five years old when he first ascended the throne, because his father, Crown Prince Carol, had left Romania and renounced all rights in favor of his son. Dissatisfied with the regency of the boy king, the Romanian government arranged for the return of Carol from exile, proclaiming him king on June 9, 1930. World War II brought economic disaster and territorial losses to Romania with Nazi Germany's encouragement of the anti-Semitic Romanian Iron Guard. A scapegoat was made of King Carol II (1893–1953) and his Jewish mistress, Magda Lupescu. Carol abdicated and left Romania with Madame Lupescu, and eighteen-year-old Michael once more became king in 1940. He was forced to resign the throne by the Moscow-trained Communists in 1947 and, like his father before him, now lives in exile.

☞ A 159.

During the American War of Independence in 1776, Louis XVI of France, defying his ministers, authorized secret aid to the beleaguered colonies. He solicited the equivalent of one million livres (French money discontinued in 1794) from the Spanish government for arms, at the same time guaranteeing that the king of Spain would not be implicated.

☞ A 160.

On that date, a presidential executive order made nondiscrimination in government employment a public policy.

☞ A 161.

The order Washington signed in November 1775 expressly forbade the recruitment of blacks during the American Revolution. He reversed the order the following month.

☞ A 162.

In each of the countries mentioned, the two celebrities died on the same day. Huxley and Kennedy died on November 22, 1963; Piaf and Cocteau on October 11, 1963; Stalin and Prokofiev on March 5, 1953.

☞ A 163.

The calligrapher Jacob Shallus. He was paid thirty dollars to copy out the Constitution in his exquisite hand, making it undoubtedly the most famous work of calligraphy in the world. He died of the same yellow fever epidemic that led to the move of the government, and the Constitution, from Philadelphia to Trenton. Shallus was forty-six years old when he died in 1796. Washington,

GENERAL HISTORY

Madison, and the thirty-seven other signatories were the founders or framers of the Constitution.

☞ A 164.

The October Revolution actually took place on October 25, 1917, according to the Julian, or Old Style, calendar in use at the time in Russia. That calendar was thirteen days behind the New Style, or Gregorian, calendar used by the Western world. The Gregorian calendar was adopted by the Soviet Union on January 26, 1918, and until 1990 the October Revolution was celebrated in November.

☞ A 165.

Neither of the two. The maritime disaster with the most casualties ever occurred during World War II, when a Soviet submarine torpedoed and sank the Nazi transport *Wilhelm Gustloff,* killing an estimated 7,700 on January 30, 1945.

☞ A 166.

The wife of President Lyndon Baines Johnson (1908–73), Lady Bird Johnson (b. 1913).

☞ A 167.

The photograph most often asked for shows President Richard M. Nixon meeting Elvis Presley (1935–77). It was taken in 1970 when the singer inquired whether he could serve as an undercover agent in the war against drugs. The second most popular picture is a shot of the *Arizona* sinking at Pearl Harbor on December 8, 1941. The third most frequently demanded photo is a portrait of President Abraham Lincoln.

☞ # A 168.

1) Both presidents were assassinated. 2) Both were shot in the head from behind. 3) They were shot on a Friday. 4) They were shot in the presence of their wives. 5) Lincoln's assassin, John Wilkes Booth, was born in 1839; Kennedy's killer, Lee Harvey Oswald, was born in 1939. 6) Lincoln's secretary was named Kennedy; Kennedy's secretary was named Lincoln. 7) Both secretaries advised their presidents not to go to the place where they were shot. 8) Abraham Lincoln was elected in 1860; John F. Kennedy came to office in 1960.

☞ # A 169.

St. Eustatius was the first foreign government to recognize American sovereignty. Its Dutch governor ordered the guns of the local garrison fired in a welcoming salvo to a ship flying the flag of the Continental Congress on November 6, 1776. From 1774 the island also served as the foremost conduit through which the American colonists obtained supplies from Europe, including a great deal of trade from British merchants. This profitable trade lasted until February 1781, when the British Admiral Sir George Brydges Rodney seized the island. By that time it had lost most of its strategic significance.

GENERAL HISTORY

☞ **A 170.**

The Jews had little reason to celebrate. Not only were they prohibited from practicing many occupations in what was then New Netherland, but the Dutch colonial governor, Peter Stuyvesant (1592–1672), did not permit them to build a synagogue in New Amsterdam. Even though the British took over New Netherland in 1664, it was not until 1727 that Jews there were able to enjoy the benefits of citizenship allowed to Jewish immigrants in other parts of the New World, particularly in New England.

☞ **A 171.**

In 1815, Congress purchased Jefferson's library of over six thousand volumes, adding these books to the then-comparatively scanty Library of Congress and changing it from a parliamentary to a general reference library. Because of this magnificent collection of books, Jefferson has been regarded ever since as the Library of Congress's virtual founder.

☞ **A 172.**

Asser Levy became the first Jewish citizen of North America, in 1657.

☞ **A 173.**

The son was "Duke" Ellington (1899–1974). His father, James Edward Ellington, worked as a butler in the

White House and later became a blueprint maker for the U.S. Navy. "Duke" himself was awarded the President's Medal for Special Merit by President Dwight D. Eisenhower, the President's Gold Medal by President Lyndon B. Johnson, and the Presidential Medal of Freedom by President Richard M. Nixon.

☞ A 174.

The ruler was Frederick I, better known as Barbarossa (c. 1123–90). At the height of his reign, he assembled a vast army to take Jerusalem from the Saracen leader Saladin (1138–93), and while crossing the River Salef he drowned. Many of his followers were so devastated by his sudden death, while engaged in a religious war, that they killed themselves; others felt that with the emperor's death, their Christian God had deserted them, that Allah was shown to be more powerful, and they converted to Mohammedanism. His son, Henry VI, died soon after and Barbarossa's grandson, Frederick II, ruled from 1196 to 1250. His rule in Germany and Italy proved a failure, and the enactments of 1220 and 1231 contributed to the disintegration of the empire and the fall of the royal house—the *Hohenstaufen.*

☞ A 175.

The emperor is Charles the Great (Charlemagne) (742–814). He helped design the now only partially extant basilica that has been incorporated into what is now the Aachen (Aix-la-Chapelle) cathedral, where he is buried. A unifier of European culture and Holy Roman Emperor of France, Germany, and Italy, he is still considered a hero by both Germany and France.

GENERAL HISTORY

☞ **A 176.**

The man was Sir William Stephenson (1896–1989), the Canadian-born spy master known as Intrepid. In 1941, he became British Security Coordinator for the Western Hemisphere, a liaison between Churchill and Roosevelt, and operated a spy network that uncovered the activities of Axis agents in South America and elsewhere. William Stevenson wrote about him in *A Man Called Intrepid,* and O.S.S. chief Major General William J. (Wild Bill) Donovan claimed that Stephenson taught every Allied agent everything they needed to know about foreign intelligence.

☞ **A 177.**

Nobody was commissioned to compose the melody to Francis Scott Key's poem, which he wrote in 1814 after he sighted the American flag over Fort McHenry following a night of heavy shelling. The tune actually was taken from a popular English song, "To Anacreon in Heaven." Even more important, "The Star-Spangled Banner" did not become the United States's official national anthem in the nineteenth century, but only when the U.S. Congress passed the necessary bill on March 3, 1931.

☞ **A 178.**

The guillotine continued to be used for executions in France until the abolition of the death penalty in 1981.

ANSWERS

☞ A 179.

This comment is supposed to have been uttered originally by Marie Antoinette, but in fact the remark already appears in *Confessions* by Rousseau (1712–78), who attributed this callous observation to an unnamed princess at least two years before Marie Antoinette even arrived in France in 1770. Marie Antoinette was the ninth child of Austria's Emperor Francis I, and after marrying the French dauphin in 1770 did not become queen of France until 1774, several years after the publication of *Confessions.*

☞ A 180.

The two presidents indeed were related. Francis Cooke and Hester De La Noye had a child in Leiden, Holland, and all three sailed on the *Mayflower* in 1620. Their daughter, Jane, was Mr. Bush's "grandmother" eleven times removed. Hester's sister, Marie De La Noye, also had a child in Leiden, named Philippe. The name De La Noye became Delano, and Philippe's grandchild, seven generations removed, was Franklin Delano Roosevelt.

☞ A 181.

That's what the world heard when astronaut Neil Armstrong (b. 1930) became the first human being to set foot on the moon. But it is not what Neil Armstrong said, as he pointed out later to the press. What he said was: "That's one small step for *a* man, one giant leap for mankind." There was so much static at the time that the article *a* was completely eliminated from the statement received on earth.

☞ A 182.

When Georg Friedrich Händel (1685–1759) was offered the post of kapellmeister to the elector of Hanover in 1709, he accepted the job but soon after spent more time in England composing and conducting than in Germany, much to the chagrin of the elector. As England's Queen Anne (1665–1714) lay dying, with none of her seventeen children surviving her, the Whigs invited the elector of the house of Hanover, George Louis, to England since he was a great-grandson of England's King James I. He became King George I (1660–1727) after Queen Anne had died. Händel was deeply ashamed and embarrassed now for having deserted his former master and did not venture to appear at court. Only at the intercession of Händel's patron, Baron Kielmansegge, a pardon was obtained, and the new English king, who spoke nothing but German, received the composer back into his good graces.

☞ A 183.

The first black governor in the United States was a former slave and Reconstruction-era politician, Pinckney Benton Stewart Pinchback. He became governor of Louisiana for four weeks in 1872 and 1873 when Governor Henry Clay Warmoth was brought before the Louisiana legislature on impeachment charges. When Mr. Warmoth's term expired during impeachment proceedings, Governor Pinchback stepped down from his caretaker role and a white man, William Pitt Kellogg, was sworn in as the new governor.

However, the first black American *elected* to serve as governor of a U.S. state, L. Douglas Wilder (b. 1931), was sworn in only in 1990 as the Democratic chief executive of Virginia.

ANSWERS

☞ A 184.

That editorial had not been written about Mikhail Gorbachev's (b. 1931) Soviet Union of the 1980s or about Boris Yeltsin's (b. 1931) Republic of Russia and the Commonwealth of Independent States, but it appeared in the *Times* in the 1930s and described the Soviet Union of Josef Stalin.

☞ A 185.

The name of the city is Gallipoli. The purpose of the Allied World War I action in February and March 1915 was to capture Turkey's capital, Constantinople, and to divert Turkish forces pressing the Russians on the Caucasus front. Failing to achieve these objectives, the Allies landed in April 1915 to secure the peninsula, but their attempts to hold the area and to advance proved to be one of the classic failures of military history, and the Allies evacuated the Gallipoli beachheads in January 1916. The Turkish hero of the peninsula and the Dardanelles was Mustapha Kemal Pasha (Atatürk) (1881–1938); his Nationalists set up a provisional government in Angora in 1920, breaking with the sultan's government in Constantinople, and after the sultan's flight in 1922 made it the new capital of Turkey in 1923. In 1930 Angora became Ankara and Constantinople was changed to Istanbul.

☞ A 186.

Catherine II (the Great) of Russia (1729–96). She reigned from 1762 (when she overthrew her husband, Peter III, in a bloodless coup), until her death. Incidentally, Peter was also born in Germany. He and Catherine tolerated each other's infidelities, but he was killed in a scuffle during dinner a few days after being overthrown in 1762, most likely by Alexis Orlov, the brother of one of Catherine's lovers.

☞ A 187.

Queen Christina of Sweden (1626–89). For many years her female "bedfellow," as she described her to the English ambassador, was Ebba Sparre (Belle de la Gardie). After it was discovered that she secretly converted to Roman Catholicism, Christina was compelled to abdicate. She tried to become queen of Poland, later queen of Naples, and twice attempted to regain the throne in Sweden. Her maxims are collected in a book called *Les Sentiments Héroiques*; the synopsis of her reign, dictated to a secretary around 1680, is titled *Mémoire de ce qui c'est passé durant le règne de la reine ajoutées par elle-même*; and she called her autobiography *Histoire de la Reine Christine fait par elle-même Rome 11 Juin 1681* (unfinished).

She asked the French philosopher Descartes to come to Sweden to instruct her, and arranged to have her philosophy lessons at five o'clock in the morning. Descartes caught a chill that led to pneumonia and died, four months after his arrival. Christina herself died of the consequences of a fit of rage when informed that one of her favorites, Angelica, was nearly raped by the Abbé Vanini. Already quite sick in Rome, she ordered the captain of her guard to bring her Vanini's head. Then she fell to the ground in a faint from which she awoke only sporadically and finally died a few days later. She also has the honor of being the only woman buried in St. Peter's. Greta Garbo portrayed her on the screen in 1933.

☞ **A 188.**

The speaker was President Woodrow Wilson. He made these statements on September 25, 1919, at Pueblo, Colorado. That night he collapsed, suffering from a thrombosis that paralyzed his left arm and leg. For two months he hovered between life and death. The president never fully recovered his health, although he regained full control of his mental faculties.

☞ **A 189.**

Nobody knows for sure, but she may have been secretly married to Grigorii Potemkin (1739–91), on whom she conferred the illustrious titles governor general of "New Russia" (Ukraine) and prince of the Holy Roman Empire, in addition to giving him a palace in St. Petersburg, even though he maintained his quarters in the Winter Palace. Catherine had known Potemkin since 1762, but their passionate affair is known to have lasted only from 1771 to 1775. In those few years she referred to him in her affectionate letters as "My dear husband," "My darling husband," "My master," and "Dear spouse." However, there are no documents to prove they were formally wed. After 1775 they no longer lived together; he introduced many reforms in the army, built a fleet in the Black Sea, and colonized the Russian steppes in the south. Catherine and Potemkin cherished each other's political and personal ties until his death in 1791.

☞ A 190.

When Christina's childhood friend Maria Euphrosyne expressed interest in Christina's own favorite, Magnuus, she gave her consent and magnanimously offered the man to Maria. Similarly, when scandal made Elizabeth's marriage to Robert Dudley impossible, she offered him to her cousin Mary Queen of Scots.

☞ A 191.

The statement was made by Thomas R. Marshall (1854–1925), President Wilson's vice president. After Wilson's paralysis in September and October 1919, Marshall was known to be terrified at the prospect of becoming president, but he said he would have made the necessary concessions with Senator Henry Cabot Lodge (1850–1924) and the Senate so that the Treaty of Versailles could have been ratified. Opposition to German nationalism and a thirst for revenge, however, made the 1919 Versailles Treaty excessively harsh and destroyed the more farsighted Fourteen Points that President Wilson had previously drawn up. The French, Italians, and Japanese insisted on territorial and economic concessions; France demanded the separation of the Saar's coal basin and steelworks from Germany; and huge German reparations were the nails in the coffin of a secure peace. Wilson's reputation had suffered to achieve a more just, secure peace, a fact further aggravated by Senator Lodge's insistence on separating the Versailles Treaty from the League of Nations, Wilson's greatest postwar achievement, and Lodge's fifteen other economic reservations about the treaty. Lodge's own version of the treaty finally won in the Senate in March

1920, opening the way to a most severe reparations pact (later to be modified by the American Dawes-Young plans as being too oppressive) to be imposed on Germany. This strict pact was used by Hitler later as a reason for starting World War II, which, ironically, Wilson had predicted in 1919.

☞ A 192.

The republic is San Marino (population 23,600), which began its history in the fourth century A.D. Although it briefly came under the control of Cesare Borgia in 1503, it has been independent for almost 1,700 years. However, it was only the 175th nation to become a full member of the United Nations, in March 1992!

☞ A 193.

Begin frequently bought weapons and explosives from the Arabs. Until the end of 1943 he served in the British army in Palestine as a conscripted interpreter.

☞ A 194.

A) Abraham Lincoln. B) Rutherford B. Hayes (1822–93), the year before he became president. C) Thomas Edison (1847–1931). D) David Lloyd George, former prime minister of Great Britain. E) Frank Knox, U.S. Secretary of the Navy. F) Adolf Hitler, in 1940.

☞ A 195.

Anthony Eden (1897–1977). Queen Elizabeth II (b. 1926) instead went to London to spare Sir Anthony the jour-

GENERAL HISTORY

ney and accepted his resignation in Buckingham Palace on January 9, 1957.

☞ A 196.

The year 1945 proved to be the most extreme British election swing to the left since the Liberal landslide of 1906 when Winston Churchill was among the *left*-wing victors.

☞ A 197.

Abraham Lincoln. For ten years, from 1846 to 1856, he belonged to the Whig party, opposing the largely proslavery Democratic party. In 1854, when the liberal wing of the Democrats refused to merge with the anti-slavery Whigs, Lincoln removed himself voluntarily from the electoral race and persuaded his backers to vote for his opponent, Lyman Trumbull, the antislavery Democrat. With the Whigs in disarray, the anti-slavery faction of the North formed a new party, the Republicans, in 1856. Lincoln joined the Republican party reluctantly, fearing that extremists would dominate it, but two years later (1858), during his famous seven joint debates with Senator Stephen A. Douglas (1813–61), he reinforced his antislavery position, declaring that a government cannot endure in a nation permanently half slave and half free and that he looked toward the ultimate extinction of slavery by preventing its spread. Douglas won the senatorship by a vote in the legislature of 54 to 46, but Lincoln became president of the United States two years later and found a loyal supporter in Douglas, who died within a few months.

WORLD WAR II AND THE NAZIS

☞ **A 1.**

The Enigma machine did not send out the Germans'
High Command decision to start Hitler's final offensive.
Hitler had begun to suspect that the Allies were on to
the Enigma's secret code, and he ordered a complete
message blackout for the offensive. Fortunately he
became suspicious about Britain's decrypting capabili-
ties quite late in the war, just before his defeat.

☞ **A 2.**

1) Those accused of the plot against Hitler were hung or
shot—roughly 3,000 of them. Five thousand more were
sentenced to death, but through bureaucratic bungling
managed to survive the war. Many of the executions
took place at the Plötzensee barracks where piano wire
was not available. They were hung from ropes on the

barracks' meat hooks, according to the director of the film department of the propaganda ministry, Fritz Hippler. These films were sent to Hitler for viewing, then destroyed. Hundreds of the accused were executed in other places, not necessarily by hanging, but there is no proof that any were hung with piano wire. All this was corroborated by cameraman Sasse and soundman Braun, who filmed the hangings.

2) Winston Churchill learned beforehand of the impending November 1940 Nazi attack on Coventry but *not* of its magnitude, which Anthony C. Brown explained in his book *Bodyguard of Lies.* The Enigma rotor code of the Germans did not bring up the matter of a *Vernichtungsangriff,* an annihilation raid, and for this reason Churchill could not use many defensive planes against the Nazis. It is true he did not want to tip off the Nazis that the British had cracked their code and thus compromise the Ultra decoder, which was perfected by the Poles Rejewski and Zygalski, the finest cryptanalysts in the world, and by British citizens Alfred Knox, Wilfred Dunderdale, and especially Alan Turing. It is a rumor, however, that the British hardly defended the city. They hurled an enormous amount of flak at the Nazi air force and could not use too many RAF fighter planes for this very reason. Moreover, the Nazis repeated an attack on Coventry in April 1941.

☞ **A 3.**

1) Yes, there was an operation named "Canned Goods." It took place on August 31, 1939, when Hitler ordered Gestapo Chief Heinrich Müller as well as Himmler and Heydrich to stage a feigned military attack on the German radio station at Gleiwitz. The man in charge of the operation was SS Colonel Alfred

Naujocks. Thirteen German concentration camp inmates from Oranienburg were dressed in Polish uniforms, injected with poison, then shot and placed in a forest near the village of Hochlinde and around the radio station, making it appear that the "Poles" were shot as they tried to storm the German radio station, which was then just across the border from Poland. One of the dead inmates was planted inside the studio while an announcement was made in Polish over the open microphones that Poland had invaded Germany. All of this was done for the benefit of the domestic and foreign press. Hitler used this fake incident as a pretext for invading Poland the following day and starting World War II. Later, Naujocks deserted to the Americans and was imprisoned by them, but he escaped and was never heard of again. Nor was Heinrich Müller.

2) Neither the Danish king nor hundreds of thousands of Danes wore the Star of David, although some did, as an expression of solidarity with Denmark's Jews. Generally, the Danes felt fiercely protective toward their Jewish citizens, so much so that during the Nazi occupation from 1940 to 1943 the Germans did not consider it profitable to interfere with the Danish Jewish population as long as the Danes complied with the Danish-German agreement signed in April 1940. Only after the Danes increased their resistance movement against the Nazis was martial law declared in September 1943. The top Nazi in Denmark, former Gestapo legal adviser Dr. Werner Best, used this opportunity to try to begin deportation proceedings against Danish Jews. Immediately the Danes started smuggling Jews to Sweden, contributing almost half the financial funds for this risky operation. Of about eight thousand Jews, around two hundred were killed by the Nazis, drowned, or committed suicide. Danish fishermen

and captains saved about 98 percent of the Danish Jews. After the war, Dr. Best served only a six-year prison sentence for his war crimes.

☞ **A 4.**

Because the British ship was transporting fifteen hundred German and Italian prisoners of war to Canada. Most of them drowned.

☞ **A 5.**

He was an Englishman named Houston Stewart Chamberlain (1855–1927). He also supported Germany in World War I and became a naturalized German citizen in 1916.

☞ **A 6.**

Hundreds of millions of dollars in currency, precious stones and metals (550,000 ounces of gold, 3,500 ounces of platinum, and 4,638 carats of diamonds), as well as hundreds of works of art were taken from more than twenty million Nazi victims and shipped in six U-boats to Argentina. Hitler's deputy, Martin Bormann, directed this 1945 German submarine operation. Four German and Argentine Nazis deposited the loot in Banco Germánico and Banco Tourquist in the name of Eva Duarte (1919–52), Juan Perón's then-mistress. All four Nazis were later murdered and none of the assailants have ever been found. The loot was confiscated and converted into Argentine currency and used for Perón's (1895–1974) political programs.

ANSWERS

☞ **A 7.**

The first person to warn the world about the outrageous assertion that the Holocaust was only Zionist propaganda was General Dwight D. Eisenhower. In a letter to Army chief of staff General George C. Marshall (1880–1959) in 1945, even before World War II ended, Eisenhower wrote about his visit to the German concentration camp in Ohrdorf: "The things I saw beggar description. The visual evidence and verbal testimony of starvation, cruelty, and bestiality were so overpowering as to leave me a bit sick. . . . I made the visit deliberately in order to be in a position to give firsthand evidence of these things if ever, in the future, there develops a tendency to charge these allegations merely to 'propaganda.' "

☞ **A 8.**

It was a secret operation in which both Germany and the United States were involved around 1947. Its aim was to help clear many German Nazi scientists—such as Wernher von Braun (1912–77) and especially Arthur Rudolph, later to become production chief for the Saturn V rocket—to get permanent immigration visas to the United States to work on rocket technology. The words *paper clip* indicated the documentation that was paper-clipped to the photos of each German scientist whom the Pentagon tried to have brought to the United States before the Soviet Union could nab them. In order to facilitate their speedy transfer from West Germany to the United States, the records of many of the German top scientists were doctored, or "sanitized," by orders of the Pentagon, to remove the stain of their ardent Nazi pasts.

WORLD WAR II AND THE NAZIS

This was especially applicable to Arthur Rudolph, whose Nazi fanaticism was well documented (but later expunged), and who used thousands of slave laborers from the concentration camp of Nordhausen to build von Braun's V-2 weapons under Hitler. Twenty thousand of the prisoners were killed or died of starvation. Most of the German scientists gained American citizenship, but Rudolph renounced his after he was deported back to Germany in 1984 because of his alleged war crimes.

☞ **A 9.**

The gypsy's name was Jean Baptiste "Django" Reinhardt (1910–53). Even today, Reinhardt is considered one of the greatest jazz guitar players of all time. He was a Tzigane gypsy, born in Belgium, who lived mostly just outside Paris. The accident that threatened to shorten his life and career was a fire in his caravan in 1928, in which he was severely burned and the fourth and fifth fingers of his left hand were completely mutilated. In spite of this seemingly insurmountable problem, he proceeded to fashion a truly remarkable technique. In Europe he was as famous as Piaf and Chevalier. In the thirties, he formed the Quintette du Hot Club de France (QHCF), featuring the great jazz violinist Stephane Grappelli. Reinhardt appeared with his Quintette at London's State Kilburn Theatre the day Chamberlain declared war on Hitler, September 3, 1939, and then immediately returned to France. He hired the clarinetist Hubert Rostaing to take the place of Grappelli, who remained in England, and openly played in Paris and other towns and occupied countries after the Nazis conquered Europe, advertising himself merely as J. Reinhardt on posters. Since the Germans wanted French collaboration and Reinhardt was respected by many German soldiers, who attended his concerts (all reference to jazz was dropped during the occupation), he was not touched by them. In fact, they considered his music part of France's heritage, not American culture. When the Allies started attacking and bombing Paris, Reinhardt spent nights in the Pigalle metro station and finally went to Thonon-les-Bains, near the Swiss border on Lake Leman, where he gave more musical performances. He was never accused of collaborating with the enemy after the war since the gypsies were on the Nazi death list. Following a fishing trip on the Seine, he died of a stroke in Samois-sur-Seine, near Fontainebleau, in May 1953. Reinhardt was illiterate and could not read music.

☞ A 10.

The *Spee* had expended most of its ammunition prior to its arrival on the Río de la Plata off Uruguay and could not be expected to face a major battle in shallow water and simultaneously force its way out. Even so, Langsdorff proposed to the Berlin admiralty that he fight his way out. However, he pointed out that his ship would almost certainly be sunk with all men on board without inflicting appreciable damage on the British naval force. Grand Admiral Raeder contacted Hitler, who insisted that the *Spee* must break its way out of Uruguayan waters. When Raeder showed Hitler a draft reply by the admiralty allowing the scuttling of the ship, provided that everything on board was destroyed first, Hitler agreed to have the message transmitted to Captain Langsdorff. Raeder was perplexed at Hitler's sudden change of mind but sent the message to the *Spee*.

After the scuttling, Hitler flew into a rage, contending that he was misunderstood; he was incensed over the fact that nothing was destroyed on the ship, due to a shortage of explosives. This enabled British intelligence to examine the battleship's radar gear. The official message for the world press meanwhile was altered, making it appear that Hitler had indeed ordered the scuttling. A short time later, Captain Langsdorff committed suicide in Buenos Aires, where the *Spee*'s crew had been sent.

☞ A 11.

The Ultra decoder could decrypt the German High Command Enigma code, including most of Hitler's and Mussolini's orders. However, the German navy under Dönitz (1891–1980) used a different Enigma machine. Not until the seizure of the German U-110 near Greenland in 1941 did the British find the encoding manuals necessary for the German navy's Enigma machine. Even this was soon of no use to the British, however, when the Nazis used a brand-new Triton code, which the British could not break until January 1943. Only by mid-1943 did the British gain on the "wolf-packs," which were discontinued at the end of May in that year. Worst of all, the Germans knew about the Allied convoy code. Only when the Allies changed their codes every month did the Nazis fail to decrypt them, and Allied losses on the Atlantic decreased sharply. The fact that the Nazis had broken the Allied convoy code was kept secret until 1966. It never received the same kind of publicity that the Allies gave to the breaking of the German Enigma code.

☞ A 12.

The British could afford to ignore Canaris's secret information, because they had broken the Nazis' Enigma machine code with their own Ultra Turing engine. The British did not reveal much about the Enigma decoder for thirty years after World War II, hoping that the Soviets would use the Enigma machine, too. But since double-spy Kim Philby worked in British intelligence during World War II, it is believed that he tipped off the Soviets about the British using Ultra after the war.

☞ A 13.

The sister of Friedrich Nietzsche (1844–1900): Elisabeth Nietzsche-Förster. She had married the virulent anti-Semite Bernhard Förster, moved with him to Paraguay, and opened a pure Christian German colony called Nueva Germania. Nietzsche abhorred the anti-Semitic views of his brother-in-law. Förster killed himself after he was discovered in a financial scandal, and Elisabeth returned to Germany to edit, alter, and misinterpret some of her brother's writings and notes—collected works for which she was nominated to receive the Nobel Prize in literature. She even forged documents regarding their father's mental illness and used Nietzsche's notes on *The Will to Power* as a representation that unscrupulously distorted Nietzsche's thoughts long after his death in 1900. That is why Hitler admired the woman and used her writings about the German philosopher to serve the aims of Nazism.

☞ A 14.

Fräulein Wessel. She was the sister of Horst Wessel (1907–30), the man originally credited with writing the Nazi party anthem, the Horst Wessel song.

WORLD WAR II AND THE NAZIS

☞ **A 15.**

Until the time that Himmler (1900–45) and his police powers in Nazi Germany became virtually absolute and invincible, Canaris fooled the Gestapo as late as the summer of 1942 by mounting an audacious rescue operation and securing exit permits for many Berlin Jews. They were represented to Gestapo headquarters as German *Abwehr* espionage agents earmarked for work as saboteurs in the United States and could leave Germany safely without interference from the Nazi government authorities.

☞ **A 16.**

While about 95 percent of German Jews were murdered by the Nazis in World War II, about 85 percent of Italian Jews in Italy *survived*. Approximately 6,000 were murdered in concentration camps. The reason for the higher percentage of survivors from Italy: Anti-Semitism has virtually never been a national issue in Italy. Also, the Italians' contempt for governmental authority can be credited with saving many Jewish lives and for such a high survival rate of Jews in Italy.

☞ **A 17.**

When Hitler was decorated with the Iron Cross, First Class, in World War I, on August 4, 1918. Hitler knew that the man who pinned it on his jacket was First Lieutenant Hugo Gutmann, a Jew.

ANSWERS

☞ **A 18.**

This was the excuse for Hitler's policies of aggression that he often stated in his speeches, and to a degree, of course, they contributed to his drive to conquer Europe. However, above everything else, what drove him, and Germany, to a new definition of a world power to be reckoned with was the proclamation by General Erich Ludendorff in the closing months of World War I. The general called for pushing Russia back a thousand kilometers, annexing Belgium and northeastern France, and turning Toulon into a German port on the Mediterranean. Far from admitting defeat, Ludendorff and his German Fatherland Party planned four months before the end of World War I to control not only its eastern neighbors but its western border zones as well. This, above all, explains Ludendorff's presence during Hitler's failed Munich Putsch of 1923 and the army's support of Adolf Hitler when he became chancellor in 1933.

☞ **A 19.**

Certainly not to the aggressiveness of the ground troops, but mostly to heavy saturation bombing and offensive tank tactics. According to S. L. A. Marshall's classic 1947 study *Men Against Fire* only about 25 percent of the American soldiers fired their rifles in that theater of war, and often not more than 15 percent. This was confirmed by E. A. Reitan, professor of history at Illinois State University. However, Reitan correctly points out that the purpose of infantry is to advance on the enemy and occupy friendly and enemy territory, regardless of whether rifles are fired or not.

WORLD WAR II AND THE NAZIS

☞ **A 20.**

Believe it or not, it was the man who led the Japanese air attack on Pearl Harbor with the war cry, "Tora! Tora! Tora!"—Commander Mitsuo Fuchida. On August 6, 1945, he was flying to Hiroshima when he saw the mushroom cloud of the atom bomb in the distance. He was also aboard the *Missouri* in September 1945, witnessing the formal surrender ceremonies. He was so great an admirer of Hitler that he sported a similar mustache. Several years after World War II, he became a convert to Christianity and often visited the United States as an evangelist. He died in 1974, at age seventy-two.

☞ **A 21.**

In February 1987, the Italian government and Jewish organizations signed an accord that replaced the anti-Semitic Mussolini-sponsored legislation that had governed Jewish life in Italy for more than four decades after the end of World War II. There are fewer than forty thousand Italian Jews living in Italy—the same number that resided there before World War II.

☞ **A 22.**

A grand total of 560,000 troops. From Dunkirk alone—366,162.

☞ **A 23.**

Yes and no. Josef Mengele—the bestial medical doctor at Auschwitz, also known as the White Angel or Angel

ANSWERS

of Death—never met Hitler, nor did Hitler ever know of anybody named Mengele performing medical experiments on Auschwitz prisoners. However, Hitler did meet Josef Mengele's father, Karl Sr. The latter played host to the Nazi leader in 1932 when Hitler gave a speech on farming in Karl Mengele's farm equipment factory near Munich. Karl had already joined the Nazi party in 1931, two years before Hitler became chancellor. The Mengele factory still exists and prospers.

☞ A 24.

It took place in 1936 and 1937 when Hitler's Luftwaffe and Mussolini's air force transported Franco's Moorish mercenaries from Africa to the mainland of Spain to fight in the Spanish civil war.

☞ A 25.

Hitler apologized to General Walter Dornberger on July 8, 1942, on hearing that rockets capable of hitting London would be operational within a year or two. Hitler conceded that he had made a mistake back in the 1930s when he did not have the confidence in Dornberger and his A-4 rocket program that was to go underway in Peenemünde on the Baltic. Among the rocket scientists was the chief architect of the V-2 rocket, thirty-year-old Wernher von Braun, whose weapon devastated parts of London in 1944 and 1945. Later he directed the United States' NASA Marshall Space Flight Center, which helped put an American—Neil Armstrong, on July 20, 1969—on the moon.

☞ **A 26.**

No. Dönitz immediately appointed Admiral Hans Georg von Friedeburg to be the new head of the Nazi navy, a post he held until May 7, 1945, when he and General Jodl signed Germany's surrender terms to the Allies in a little red schoolhouse in Reims. Soon after that, von Friedeburg killed himself.

☞ **A 27.**

Yes. At the end of May 1945, 17,000 Cossacks were handed over by the Allies to the Soviet forces at Judensburg, Austria. Stalin had most of them sentenced to death and the rest shipped to Siberia. During World War II these Cossacks had defected to Hitler's side, many joining SS divisions and the Russian National Liberation Army (RONA). They were known to be virulently anti-Semitic, but they also joined the anti-Soviet German forces under General-Major Helmuth von Panwitz in order to gain independence for their land from Stalin and Moscow, never realizing that they were serving only German Nazi aims.

☞ **A 28.**

Hitler admired his Axis partner Benito Mussolini for his brutal tactics (including gas warfare) in crushing the Abyssinians in 1936. What really influenced Hitler in putting Mussolini in the secondary role of the Axis was the Italians' poor performance during military maneuvers that Hitler attended in May 1938 outside Santa Marinella near Rome. Even more important, Mussolini

ANSWERS

played an increasingly insignificant role in the Axis after he declared war on France and Great Britain on June 10, 1940, since his Fascist armies were defeated by the Allies in virtually every military campaign thereafter.

☞ **A 29.**

The country is Finland. In spite of a Finnish-Soviet nonaggression pact, signed in 1932, the Soviets (who were allied with Hitler's government) made territorial demands on Finland in 1939 and then launched a military campaign when Finland resisted these demands. Field Marshal Mannerheim's Finns fought heroically for 105 days, then had to sue for peace and cede more than one-tenth of Finnish territory to the Soviet Union. In order to recover their own land, they let Hitler use part of their country to launch his invasion against the Soviet Union. The Finns never became military allies of the Nazis, however. Although they had to pay reparations to Moscow after the war, they were again independent and set up their own democratic government, which stands to this day.

☞ **A 30.**

It was not the bad weather or the objections from his generals. Hitler was determined to invade the Low Countries in October 1939, but a Luftwaffe major carrying the invasion plans in his briefcase crash-landed in fog in a new Messerschmitt scout plane in Belgium. As a result, Belgian authorities found themselves in the possession of the entire German invasion plan. However, they were not certain that this was not a German trick, and they did nothing about it. Even so, Hitler did not know what the Allies were going to do about the disclosure, and he and his generals had to rethink their entire strategy. They changed their original plan to launch a frontal assault by Army Group B on the Low Countries with a secondary attack in the Ardennes by Army Group A to a strong armored offensive through the supposedly impenetrable Ardennes in the spring of 1940.

☞ A 31.

Martin Luther (no relation to the founder of the Reformation).

☞ A 32.

Which item is false? Hard as it is to believe, all three of them are true.

1) The out-and-out Nazi was a man named Major Erich Hartmann. He destroyed more Allied pilots in World War II than any other pilot, chalking up 352 aerial victories, a record for any air ace in any war. He spent ten years in Soviet captivity after the war, but then the British and American government authorities used him to build up the West German Luftwaffe under NATO command. He frequently visited the United States and England as a confidential air force adviser in the 1960s and 1970s.

2) After Erich Hartmann had shot down more than three hundred enemy planes, most of them on the Russian front, Hitler invited him to his military headquarters at Rastenburg. Hartmann unbuckled his belt, to which his pistol was holstered, and hung it on a clothes hanger. When Hitler invited him to stay for lunch in another room, Hartmann returned to the clothes

hanger and buckled on his belt and pistol again without the slightest murmur of protest from Hitler. The Nazi leader obviously felt that he could trust a man who had destroyed so many enemy planes in the defense of Nazi Germany.

3) The above meeting took place on August 25, 1944, four weeks after the attempt on Hitler's life on July 20. On that August occasion, Hitler admitted to Erich Hartmann that the war was militarily lost for Nazi Germany; he also asserted that the Western powers would always be enemies of the Soviet Union. Hartmann felt that more enemy bombers could have been destroyed if young pilots had attacked them only in good weather instead of in all weather, as Hitler had demanded. Hitler simply attacked his generals as liars, then praised Hartmann and another Nazi pilot hero, H. U. Rudel, for their courage.

☞ A 33.

The monarchist coup is known as the Kapp Putsch and it took place from March 13 to 17, 1920. Even though the right-wing movement led by Captain Ehrhardt (not by Kapp) supported workers' demands to a large degree, it collapsed as a result of a general strike of the trade unions. Labor refused to work in the factories or fight on the streets. Dr. Wolfgang Kapp (1858–1922), a mediocre politician of the right (who happened to be born in New York) was installed in office. When a boy hooted at the German soldiers involved in the coup, the soldiers clubbed the boy to death. The striking trade union workers were so enraged at this brutal act that they turned against the soldiers and forced them to leave the German capital. An ironic sidelight: Another right-wing coup, led by Gustav von Kahr (1862–1934), took place at the same time in Munich; this one was successful, attracting all those determined to overthrow the Republic and repudiate the Versailles Treaty. The liaison officer engaged by the army to coordinate the two military revolts was an unknown former corporal, then unemployed, by the name of Adolf Hitler. The Kapp Putsch turned Hitler irrevocably against the trade unions. In 1934, Hitler had Kahr sentenced to death, since Kahr was responsible for crushing Hitler's 1923 putsch.

☞ A 34.

The August–September 1942 battle of Guadalcanal. Japanese troops controlled the sea at night and landed reinforcements around Guadalcanal in the dark, preventing all American movement. By day, the situation was reversed and the United States dominated the air, enabling it to land all kinds of supplies and manpower, mostly Marines, under the protection of fighter aircraft from Henderson Field. It was the beginning of the battle of the Eastern Solomons.

☞ A 35.

Hitler handed his note to General-Oberst Krebs on April 24. Krebs gave it to Lieutenant Heinz Heuer, whom he had decorated with the Knight's Cross on April 22 for seizing some Soviet maps and documents. The note was to be rushed to General Steiner with the order to attack and destroy the Soviet forces in Berlin. However, Heuer was captured by members of the Soviet army. He stuffed the message into his mouth and swallowed it. The Soviets had Heuer dig his own grave, then offered him a last cigarette. While he was smoking it, a German military barrage sent the Soviets running for cover and gave Heuer an opportunity to escape certain death. In a matter of minutes, Heuer was recaptured and sent to Siberia. Later he was asked to work for the secret police in East Berlin. Eventually, Heuer fled to West Germany and became a consultant with the British military police. Thus, General Steiner never knew of the existence of Hitler's April 24 message, although Field Marshal Keitel, after leaving Hitler's bunker on April 25, conveyed Hitler's new order to him two days later. But Generals Steiner and Henrici were swept toward the Allied lines and in no position to advance on Nauen as directed. Three days later, on April 30, Hitler shot himself.

☞ A 36.

Nazi U-boats and battleships sank almost eight million tons of Allied ships in 1942. To offset this huge loss, nearly the same amount was built in that fateful year. The second reason for Britain's survival in 1942 was that despite Nazi Admiral Dönitz's pleas to engage more U-boats in the North Atlantic that year, Hitler diverted a large number of them to the Mediterranean at a crucial moment. It was probably the only time that Hitler was instrumental in helping to save the free world from his own nefarious aims.

☞ A 37.

The *Graf Zeppelin* flew along the coast of England in order to intercept and record British radar transmissions for later analysis. The flight's goal was not accomplished because of a technical failure. The date, August 2, 1939, is of historical interest, however, because it marked the first electronic intelligence mission ever flown.

☞ A 38.

Yes, President Roosevelt knew about Japan's plans for Pearl Harbor, but he did not know the date. The person who informed him in January 1941 was the U.S. ambassador to Japan, Joseph C. Grew, only four weeks after Japanese Admiral Yamamoto first disclosed his plan to attack Pearl Harbor to the Japanese High Command. Official U.S. government circles ignored this warning (just as Stalin ignored Churchill's warning that Hitler was going to invade the Soviet Union), since Japanese novelists had used the theme of attacking Pearl Harbor for many years (for instance, in the 1933 novel *An Account of the Future War Between Japan and the United States* by Lieutenant Commander Kyusuke Fukunaga) and the United States ridiculed such a bold plan. Ironically, Admiral Kimmel (1882–1968), the highest-ranking U.S. navy officer stationed at Pearl Harbor on December 7, 1941, was handed Grew's dispatch (paraphrased by the Office of Naval Intelligence) on February 1, 1941, ten months before the attack. Although Roosevelt considered Pearl Harbor a *possible* target, he, Kimmel, and others thought it less likely to be attacked by Japan than alternative sites in the Pacific.

☞ A 39.

The *Buchanan* was one of fifty U.S. destroyers loaned to Great Britain in 1940. Although she was renamed HMS *Campbeltown,* the British still referred to her affectionately as "Old Buck." Early in 1942, her four vertical stacks were replaced with two raked-back stacks to resemble German torpedo boats of the *Möwe* class. The entire ship was fitted with twenty-four depth charges by Lieutenant Nigel Tibbets, turning her into a floating time bomb. It was the captain's (Lieutenant Commander Samuel H. Beattie) responsibility to guide the ship over the mud banks and slam her into the dry-dock caisson at the Nazi submarine pens of Saint-Nazaire in occupied France on March 28, 1942. Tibbets activated the time-bomb fuse at 11 o'clock the night before—March 27—about ten hours before the expected detonation.

When the Germans started attacking the British fleet accompanying "Old Buck" with guns, Beattie coolly signaled the Germans: "Friendly forces being fired upon." The attack stopped for an hour. Then the firing started in earnest, inflicting heavy damage and many casualties. The *Campbeltown* increased speed, then plowed into the Saint-Nazaire lock gates at 1:34 A.M. on March 28 and remained wedged there until the following morning. The commandoes on board fled ashore through enemy fire, and the Germans were convinced they had won the battle. They had killed and seized 31 Royal Navy officers, 151 seamen, 34 commando officers, and 178 enlisted commandoes, a staggering British defeat. The Nazis were elated . . . until 10:30 A.M., when "Old Buck" blew up. The dry dock was largely destroyed and could not be reopened until the early 1950s. This was Churchill's key objective—not, as is commonly assumed, the destruction of the submarine pens. Because this happened to Hitler's largest, best-equipped dry dock for battleships up to 85,000 tons, the old U.S. destroyer can be credited for shortening World War II singlehandedly.

WORLD WAR II AND THE NAZIS

☞ **A 40.**

The man credited originally with writing the Nazi party anthem, Horst Wessel, was not killed by the Communists, but by the Nazi Ali Hoehler, whose girlfriend, a prostitute named Erna Jaenecke, Wessel had stolen. (Some Hitler biographies, however, maintain that Hoehler may have been a member of the German Communist party.) Wessel wrote the lyrics of the piece, and the music is a composite of several other songs he had composed. But after Wessel was fatally wounded in the mouth by Hoehler's shot, Propaganda Minister Goebbels created the legend in his newspaper, *Der Angriff,* that Wessel was wounded by Communists. For five weeks Wessel actually knew of his own fictitious martyrdom before he died on February 23, 1930. The many songs found in his apartment were hastily pieced together at Hitler's order, and the result became the Nazi party's anthem. Both Ali Hoehler and the prostitute Jaenecke died mysteriously a few weeks after Wessel's death.

Incidentally, today nobody knows who patched together the musical composition from several of Wessel's songs, although a former friend of Hitler's, "Putzi" Hanfstaengl, wrote that the melody was "exactly that of a Vienna cabaret song at the turn of the century."

☞ **A 41.**

There were two terrible cases in particular: On the night of January 11, 1941, a bomb exploded in the ticket hall of the Bank underground station. A total of one hundred and eleven victims were recovered, although it is likely that many bodies were never found. The other

ANSWERS

tragedy took place on October 14, 1941, at the Balham underground station when a bomb smashed through the road, killing sixty-four people taking shelter there.

☞ **A 42.**

No, not when Hitler became dictator of Nazi Germany. Later—much later. The salute was imposed only nine months before the war ended in Europe—on August 4, 1944; ten years *after* Hitler became absolute ruler following Hindenburg's death, and about nine months before his own suicide.

☞ **A 43.**

His grueling schedule, tailored to suit the work habits of Hitler and Himmler, caused Karl Wolff to suffer from kidney ailments. He had to stay with Hitler until the Führer went to bed at five in the morning, and then he had to be ready for Himmler, who started work at that hour. At best, he could only take small naps in between at irregular intervals when his two masters had no immediate need of him. Moreover, suffering from weak kidneys, he did not get special dispensation to relieve himself when on duty with Hitler or Himmler. Wolff's kidneys deteriorated so much that in February 1943 Dr. Karl Gebhardt had to operate on them. However, Wolff's efforts to shorten World War II did not reduce the fighting in Europe by a single day.

☞ **A 44.**

Both reasons apply. Hitler's policy, however, was merely a continuation of that exemplified by the March

3, 1918, Soviet-German Treaty of Brest-Litovsk, which had secured the Ukraine for Germany. This was reinforced by the German-Soviet Supplementary Treaty of August 28, 1918, which tried to make unoccupied Russia economically dependent on the Reich. Thus, Hitler's vision, espoused in *Mein Kampf,* of erecting a German Eastern Empire reflected not only his own wish for additional *Lebensraum* (living space), but also concurred with historical fact.

☞ A 45.

World War II saw many such glider operations, especially during invasions by the Allies and the Nazis. The first and most dramatic major glider operation took place early in World War II, in May 1940, when the Germans captured what was considered to be the strongest fort in the world—Fort Eben Emael in Belgium. Captain Walter Koch and his 424 men used forty-two gliders and seized the fort and nine installations in under fifteen minutes. Soon after, Belgium capitulated.

☞ A 46.

General Maxwell D. Taylor (1901–87). He parachuted with the 101st Airborne Division into Normandy on D day, June 6, 1944.

☞ A 47.

It was the sanctuary in Amsterdam where Anne Frank (1929–45) and her family lived in hiding for about two years, in a back room above her father's business. Miep Gies (Miep Van Santen in Anne's diary), who with her husband, Jan (Henk in the diary), had helped the Franks until their discovery by the Gestapo, spotted and hid Anne's diary in 1944. Nobody knows who betrayed the Franks to the Nazis for 7½ guilders per Jew. Anne's mother was killed at Auschwitz, and she and her sister were taken to the Bergen-Belsen death camp, where Anne died of typhus at age fifteen, three months before the war ended. Herr Frank was the only family member to survive. Each year, tens of thousands of tourists visit the attic where the Franks tried to wait out the war.

☞ A 48.

Hitler was supposed to have replied: "Who still talks nowadays of the extermination of the Armenians by the Turks?" (That genocide took place between 1915 and 1922.) However, the question was never asked. First of all, nobody in his right mind would have dared to ask him such a question. Second, while Hitler was alive, nobody knew that the number of Jews killed by the Nazis in World War II came to six million. According to Albert Speer, any matter relating to Jews was not discussed in Hitler's presence. Only one person—Henriette von Schirach, the wife of Baldur von Schirach (1907–74), the Reich representative in Vienna—broached the subject once. Hitler icily defended his policy toward the Jews without mentioning the death camps, but banished her forever from his presence. However, he did bring up the subject of the Armenians when addressing his generals at the Obersalzberg on August 22, 1939, shortly after von Ribbentrop had signed his nonaggression pact with the Soviets. He declared that after his seizure of Poland he would exterminate every Polish man, woman, and child. It was at that juncture that he brought up the matter of the Armenian genocide.

☞ **A 49.**

On December 7, 1941, the Japanese flew over Hawaii's third-largest island, Oahu, and attacked the American naval station at Pearl Harbor, officially bringing the United States into World War II. An equally ghastly event took place at the same hour, shortly before seven in the morning, several thousand miles away, in Kulm, the German name for the Polish town of Chelmno. Here, in a Nazi extermination camp (Kulmhof), the Germans, starting with gas vans, successfully performed their very first gassing operation, killing dozens of Jews in a type of gas chamber that was then introduced into other Nazi death camps and later "perfected." Ironically, Kulm's municipal laws in 1233 served as the foundation and prototype for civic rights in the German state of Prussia.

☞ **A 50.**

When Hitler invaded the Low Countries after the fall of Denmark and Norway, Winston Churchill was not prime minister yet, and he knew nothing about this date. But Prime Minister Neville Chamberlain knew that Hitler was going to invade Holland, Belgium, and Luxemburg on May 10, 1940, and France a few days later. This date was given to the Dutch military attaché in Berlin by Colonel Hans Oster, chief of staff of Admiral Wilhelm Canaris's *Abwehr* (Hitler's intelligence bureau of the German armed services). In spite of their top positions,

ANSWERS

both Canaris and Oster transmitted many secrets to the Allies because of their hatred for the Nazis. The Dutch military attaché forwarded the information to London, but the warning was not given sufficient weight in Whitehall, since previous warnings of a Nazi offensive had proved false because Hitler had frequently postponed it. By the time Churchill became England's prime minister on May 10, 1940, it was too late to act on it. Five years later, on April 9, 1945, both Canaris and Oster were executed by the Nazis, following the abortive bomb plot against Hitler in July 1944.

☞ A 51.

The greatest irony was that Klaus Barbie was provided with false travel documents by a Jew—a young American officer, twenty-three-year-old Leo Hecht. However, Hecht was ordered by higher-ups to give Barbie these papers, even though the Counter-Intelligence Corps knew about his war crimes.

☞ A 52.

The country was Finland. Washington broke diplomatic relations with it on June 30, 1944. It did not declare war on Finland because the Finns were forced to ally themselves with Hitler and let him use part of their country to launch the invasion of the Soviet Union in order to recover the part of Finland that the Soviets had been occupying illegally since 1940. A couple of months after the United States broke diplomatic relations with Finland, President Mannerheim (1867–1951) signed an armistice with America's wartime ally, the Soviet Union, in September 1944.

☞ # A 53.

The cynical ditty was: "If at first you don't concede—fly, fly again!" Hitler was anything but happy with the Munich agreement in 1938. He would have preferred Chamberlain's disagreement with his takeover of the Sudetenland so that he could use his Nazi troops to conquer all of Czechoslovakia. He finally did use the German army to annex the rest of Czechoslovakia in March 1939. However, Hitler did not conquer the entire country, since parts of it had been ceded to Poland and Hungary after the Munich agreement.

☞ # A 54.

As far as is known, Finland did not hand over a single Jew to the German Nazi occupation forces. Admittedly, only about 1 percent of the Finnish population was Jewish in the early 1940s, but this still meant saving several thousand Jews. The three other European countries that heroically tried to save their Jewish populations were Bulgaria, Denmark, and Norway. However, although virtually no Bulgarian Jews were deported by the Nazis, about 11,000 Jews were rounded up by the police under Bulgarian authority in Macedonia (Yugoslavia) and Thrace (Greece), which the Bulgarian forces had occupied during the war.

☞ # A 55.

The report is false. It originated because only four of the thousands of Allied troops who risked their lives to get the weapons to the Soviet Union were awarded medals. The Order of Lenin was awarded to four British

RAF pilots for their valor and determination in flying Hurricane fighter planes to the vital northern port of Murmansk in the early 1940s.

☞ A 56.

Italy. Fascist Italy declared war on England in 1940, and after Mussolini's downfall, Italy made a formal declaration of war against Nazi Germany. Although Romania declared war on the United States on December 12, 1941, Romania's King Michael did not formally declare war on Nazi Germany after Romania's Fascist dictator Antonescu was overthrown on August 23, 1944, even though Romanians briefly fought German troops in 1944.

☞ A 57.

The country was Thailand. The United States realized that the Japanese, by returning many French-occupied territories to Thailand, pressured the country to side with Japan. At the same time the Thai ambassador to the United States organized a movement to free Thailand from the Japanese, with 90,000 guerrillas fighting the Japanese invaders throughout their World War II occupation.

☞ A 58.

January 30. On that day President Roosevelt was born (1882), Hitler became chancellor of Germany (1933), and the world said farewell to Sir Winston Churchill at his funeral (1965).

☞ **A 59.**

Prime Minister Churchill said: "After all, this new bomb is just going to be bigger than our present bombs. It involves no difference in the principles of war." Neither Churchill nor Hitler at first fully grasped the consequences of atomic energy being released on the human race.

☞ **A 60.**

American journalist Joseph Kingsbury-Smith watched Streicher (1885–1946) and the other Nazi war criminals being hanged. He asked the sergeant who was in charge of the hangings why Streicher was the only one to groan when he fell through the trap. The sergeant explained that after Streicher's last words on the gallows—a shrieking "Heil Hitler!"—he adjusted the noose of the hangman's rope in such a way that the knot was not at the back of the neck but at the side. This caused Streicher to slowly strangle to death, which in turn caused the groaning sound.

☞ **A 61.**

The U.S. government seriously debated whether further military aid should be given to Great Britain lest it eventually fall into German hands. Roosevelt's special assistant, Harry Hopkins (1890–1946), later told Churchill that after the Royal Navy attacked the French naval units at Oran, President Roosevelt was convinced that Britain meant to go on fighting and was worth the risk of continued American assistance.

ANSWERS

☞ **A 62.**

Not only did the Nazis permit the International Red Cross to visit and inspect one of its concentration camps, but the Red Cross unwittingly passed along the Nazis' propaganda. Before the visit, the Nazis had spruced up their Theresienstadt (Terezin) concentration camp in Czechoslovakia—they built brand-new barracks, painted the children's facilities, and formed a large orchestra—and the Red Cross inspectors gave their blessings to the sham and reported that the Nazis treated their prisoners most generously. Since the Jewish prisoners did not fall into the Red Cross categories of prisoners of war or civilian-internees, the Jews were not given even the barest assistance, such as food packages or clothing. The Nazis filmed the camp, showing the inmates reading in the library, while the newsreel announcer commented that the Jews were having a wonderful vacation while German soldiers were dying on the eastern front. It was not mentioned, however, that all filmed inmates, including the children, were sent to Auschwitz in the next transport and gassed there. The motion picture—*The Führer Grants the Jews a Town*—was filmed in July and August 1944 for the summer visit of the Red Cross, but the film was never shown publicly in Nazi Germany. Parts of it are stored in the Yad Vashem archive in Jerusalem.

☞ **A 63.**

In a secret pact with the Soviet Union, Germany established the school at the Lipetsk spa about 500 miles east of Moscow.

☞ **A 64.**

The Nazi was Hitler's deputy, Rudolf Hess. He was never convicted of the crime of having participated in the aborted November 1923 putsch, having escaped to Austria. After Hitler was imprisoned in Landsberg, following the March 1924 trial, Hess returned from Austria and voluntarily joined his Führer in prison. It was there that Hitler dictated *Mein Kampf* to his new secretary, Rudolf Hess.

☞ **A 65.**

Hitler was never elected but appointed by President Paul von Hindenburg (1847–1934) to become chancellor of Germany on January 30, 1933.

☞ **A 66.**

The *Anschluss* that the League of Nations prevented was not Hitler's 1938 *Anschluss* but the 1931 *Anschluss,* which has been eliminated from virtually all history books. In March 1931 a free Austria had voted 90 percent in favor of merging with its German neighbor, but Germany had its hands full with Nazi and Communist rebellions and did not react to the Austrians' choice one way or another. To force the point, the Austrian government issued a publication of a project for a German-Austrian customs union on March 21, 1931. The French government and its allies protested vehemently, claiming that a customs union involved infringement of Austrian sovereignty and violated obligations assumed by the Austrian government. Faced with the threat of having to take the case before the World Court at the Hague, Ger-

ANSWERS

many and Austria voluntarily renounced the project on September 3, 1931. Just before this merger was vetoed, German Chancellor Heinrich Brüning (1885–1970) announced in June 1931 that the German people would not accept such a catastrophe and would turn to another leader. They did, nineteen months later—to Adolf Hitler.

☞ A 67.

He personally spared the life of the Jewish daughter-in-law of his favorite contemporary German composer, Richard Strauss (1864–1949).

☞ A 68.

The city is Budapest. When the Soviet army occupied Hungary's capital in 1945, there were 120,000 Jews still living in that city. Approximately 437,000 Hungarian Jews had already been sent by the Nazis to death camps and the 230,000 Jews living in Budapest were earmarked for immediate deportation when Sweden's Raoul Wallenberg arrived there in 1944. By issuing to them tens of thousands of redesigned Swedish protective passports—the *Schutzpass*—Wallenberg forced the Nazis to let many Jews remain in Budapest since they were now considered to be Swedish citizens. After the Soviets "liberated" Budapest in 1945, they arrested Wallenberg at once and sent him to his death in the Soviet Union.

☞ A 69.

It is not a rumor. Two Jewish women were indeed members of the German Nazi sports team during the 1936 Olympic Games in Berlin. One was Helene Meyer (often spelled Mayer). Already at the age of seventeen she had won the gold medal for fencing during the 1928 Olympics. A year after Hitler came to power she emigrated to the United States and studied international law in California. Although only her father was Jewish, she was considered a *Mischling* under the 1934 Nuremberg racial laws and thrown out of all German sports clubs. Hitler promised her full Aryan classification if she returned to Germany for the games as a representative of the German fencing team. She did, won the silver medal for Nazi Germany in the foil, and gave the Nazi salute on the winners' rostrum. However, the main reason she went back to Nazi Germany was to see her mother, who suffered from diabetes, she claimed, and could not obtain an exit visa to the United States.

The other Jew was Gretel Bergmann, who had emigrated to England and in 1934 had already won the English championship in the high jump. She too was offered Aryan citizenship and returned to Berlin. In the tryouts, she was easily the best high jumper among German women, but minutes before the actual Olympic contest in the stadium she backed out, and only two German women, instead of the three listed, participated in the high-jump event. They lost. The winner was a Hungarian woman who cleared 1.60 meters. In the tryouts, Gretel Bergmann had won easily with 1.64 meters. She returned at once to England. One irony: The fencer who won the gold medal over Helene Meyer also was a Hungarian, Ilona Schacherer-Elek, who was, at twenty-nine, the oldest female winner at the Berlin Olympics. The irony was that she was also Jewish.

☞ A 70.

Not Winston Churchill. In the exact phrasing of his grim address, he stated that he had nothing to offer to the

ANSWERS

British people but "blood and toil, sweat and tears."
The date of the speech in the House of Commons was
May 13, 1940.

☞ A 71.

Heinrich Himmler personally bestowed the rank of honorary general of the SS on Richard Strauss. This was done not so much to honor the composer as to add luster to the SS and to have the world acknowledge that Himmler's elite organization was representative of German culture.

☞ A 72.

The Baltic states never voluntarily joined the Soviet Union. A secret protocol signed between Berlin and Moscow on August 23, 1939, assigned Estonia, Latvia, and part of Romania to the Soviet sphere of influence, and another secret protocol signed on September 28, 1939, also transferred Lithuania to the Soviets. Both original treaties were destroyed later by the Nazis and Communists. Moscow has often denied the existence of such secret agreements. But one of Hitler's interpreters, Carl von Loesch, made microfilm copies of the protocols and buried them near Mühlhausen, where he handed them to the British and American authorities on May 14, 1945. All the protocols secretly filmed by von Loesch are authentic and their validity has never been questioned. The originals were destroyed on Nazi Foreign Minister von Ribbentrop's (1893–1946) orders in 1944.

The forced incorporation of the three Baltic republics into the Soviet Union rather than their being placed under Stalin's "sphere of influence," as the secret agreements stipulated, infuriated Hitler, as did the subsequent Soviet seizure of Bessarabia and North Bukovina (Romania), which brought the Soviet air force within striking distance of the Ploesti oil fields, Nazi Germany's main source of fossil fuels. This caused the Austrian-born dictator to order immediate preparations for the invasion and conquest of the Soviet Union, a long-held dream of his.

☞ A 73.

The event was not the U.S. atomic bombing of Hiroshima three days earlier, which was barely discussed during the Japanese cabinet meeting. A top secret study concluded that the decisive factor for surrendering to the Allies was the Soviet Union's August 8, 1945, decision to invade Japanese-held Manchuria. The Japanese leaders had sought to prevent this at any cost and regarded this as an utter catastrophe. In fact, just a few weeks earlier, Prince Konoye was named as Japanese envoy to Moscow to ask the Soviet Union to use its good offices to end the war. On August 9, 1945, the emperor set everything in motion to sue for peace. It was also the day the second atomic bomb was dropped on Japan, this time on Nagasaki. However, the Japanese had ample opportunity to surrender, not only after the first atomic bomb had been dropped, but immediately following the issuance of an ultimatum by Truman, Churchill, and Stalin at the Potsdam Conference, two weeks prior to Hiroshima, calling for the Japanese to lay down their arms. The Japanese responded with the word *mokusatsu,* which meant that they were reserving comment, but the Allied translators mistakenly interpreted the word as meaning that the Japanese were ignoring the ultimatum. This "reply" incensed President Truman. He wanted the Japanese to surrender to the Americans before the Soviet plan to attack Manchuria could be activated. Truman did not trust Stalin and decided to hasten the end of the war by using the atomic bomb.

☞ A 74.

Of just over 50,000 medical doctors in Germany before 1933, 80 percent were *not* Jewish. There were about 10,000 Jewish doctors and 42,000 non-Jewish doctors treating a nation of 66 million citizens.

☞ A 75.

This comment has been attributed to Göring, Himmler, and other Nazi bigshots. But the line actually was written by Hanns Johst, an unsuccessful German playwright who became the president of the Reich Theater Chamber. He made this statement and incorporated it in his 1933 drama *Schlageter.*

☞ A 76.

False. But he did so only when it was strategically desirable. In the summer of 1944 he ordered his Army Group South-Ukraine to withdraw from Galatz on the Danube to the Carpathian Mountains because it would make it easier for the Germans to defend themselves against the Soviets. A short time later he decided to abandon most of Greece, notably the Peloponnesus, to enemy troops, shifting his army to northern Greece to prevent the Bulgarians from seizing the railroad line for the

Allies since this was the only transportation link between Bulgaria and Greece.

☞ A 77.

Yes. When Field Marshal Hans von Kluge realized that the war was lost for Hitler in August 1944, he and his staff officer, Major Behr, tried to arrange for a meeting with U.S. General George S. Patton, Jr. (1885–1945). But when an Allied fighter-bomber destroyed von Kluge's only radio truck, he could not keep the rendezvous. Lieutenant Colonel George R. Pfann, secretary of General Patton's Third Army general staff, explained in 1945 that in August 1944 Patton attempted to make contact with the Germans, who never showed up, and von Kluge's son-in-law, Dr. Udo Esch, reported to the U.S. Counter-Intelligence Corps on July 27, 1945, that the field marshal had discussed with him surrendering the western front to the Americans in August 1944. When arrangements for the fateful meeting (of which Hitler was apprised on August 31) collapsed, von Kluge wrote a farewell letter of Nazi fanaticism and unquestioning loyalty to Hitler, then committed suicide on August 18, 1944, with the cyanide his son-in-law had given him.

☞ A 78.

Although Hermann Göring (1893–1946) was the head of the Luftwaffe, Hitler actually ordered Field Marshal Erhard Milch to secretly build the Luftwaffe in 1933, since Milch had been the founder of Lufthansa Airlines. Rumors were spread that Milch was not pure Aryan, but they were instigated to overshadow any suspicion of the embarrassing fact that he was the offspring of the incestuous relationship between his mother and her uncle. Hitler had Milch fired in 1944 over the Me-262 jet fighter—he had ordered the manufacture of jet *bombers.*

☞ **A 79.**

By the Nazis in March 1945. Nebe was found hiding in Berlin, having been a suspect of the 1944 plot against Hitler.

☞ **A 80.**

After Hitler's suicide in Berlin (April 30, 1945), the last German capital of World War II and the seat of the Nazi government was the small town of Flensburg, in the far north of Schleswig-Holstein, near the Danish frontier. Here the new, and last, Führer, Grand Admiral Karl Dönitz, was ensconced in the marine-school house at Flensburg-Mürwik. Even though Dönitz was busy arranging the capitulation of German forces on all fronts, Reichsführer SS Himmler begged him constantly for almost a week to continue the war and to form a new Werwolf Association to fight the Allies underground; when that mad scheme was rejected, he tried to convince Dönitz to become Ribbentrop's successor as the foreign minister in a new Nazi government to be headed by Himmler himself. All this was in spite of the fact that Himmler had contacted the Allies about a surrender while Hitler was still alive. However, Dönitz immediately appointed Count Lutz Schwerin von Krosigk as the new foreign minister, and Himmler finally saw that the game was up for him. He was arrested by British forces two weeks later, carrying false papers ridiculously made out for Heinrich Hitzinger, who was a member of the Secret Field Gendarmerie, a branch of the Gestapo. That identification gave him away and he confessed who he was. On May 23, 1945, while being searched in the Ülznerstrasse interrogation center in Lüneburg, he bit his potassium cyanide capsule and died within minutes. Dönitz and the last Nazi "cabinet" were arrested by the British the same day, May 23, in Flensburg.

POLITICAL WORLD

☞ **A 1.**

The two countries that refused Hitler's request to turn over any of their German Jewish refugees were his Axis partner Japan and Franco's Spain. Many of the Jewish escapees trying to find sanctuary in the other countries were refused refuge and returned to Nazi Germany and the death camps.

☞ **A 2.**

Whatever the answer, it is both right and wrong. Americans in power at the turn of the eighteenth century were either Federalists or anti-Federalists. In 1792 the Democratic party began supporting Jefferson's views. But it was popularly known as the Republican or Democratic-Republican party. *Republican* actually stood for a Democrat from the republic as opposed to the British monarchy. Except for 1825 through 1829, during John Quincy Adams's administration, this party proved to be the strongest force in Congress when Jefferson gave it direction on becoming president in 1801. Madison became one of its leaders, but not until Andrew Jackson entered the White House in 1829 was the term *Republican* dropped altogether and the Democratic party as we know it today was officially instituted. One anecdotal note: When the Democrats took control of the House of Representatives in 1913 somebody attached the Democratic party label to Madison's name in the *Biographical Directory of the American Congress*.

☞ **A 3.**

Definitely not. At the end of June 1940, Churchill was fighting alone against Hitler and for two months had been appealing to President Roosevelt for the loan of fifty destroyers in exchange for bases in the West Indies. Roosevelt's full cabinet agreed with the proposal. Fearing that the swap would be defeated in Congress because of strong isolationist influence, Roosevelt tried to bypass the legislative body. Those Americans polled by Gallup at the time voted 62 percent in favor of the swap, which was fully reported in the press. The Republican opponent, Wendell Willkie (1892–1944), and the Senate minority leader, Joe Martin, supported the deal. President Reagan, on the other hand, evaded Congress, ignored his cabinet, including his secretary of state, George Shultz (b. 1920), violated his own warnings to America's allies never to deal with terrorists and Iran, and finally came up with a bargain that was rejected by every American public opinion poll.

ANSWERS

☞ **A 4.**

The purpose of the division at the 38th parallel was to facilitate the surrender of Japanese troops in Korea— some to the Soviets, the remainder to the Western Allies—and not to divide that country into two permanent zones of occupation. Democratization procedures in 1946 and 1947, however, failed, since the Soviets would permit a unified Korea only on their own terms. Free elections were held in South Korea under the supervision of the U.N. Temporary Commission on May 10, 1948, but by that time North Korea's Soviet puppet Kim Il-sung had already established a provisional government in the north and on September 9, 1948, the Democratic People's Republic proclaimed Kim premier of North Korea—in spite of the Soviets' promise of December 27, 1945, to create a free unified Korea. Thus the two zones became a permanent fixture on the world's maps.

☞ **A 5.**

They were copied to a large extent from the U.S. Constitution.

☞ **A 6.**

The entrance of the Turks into World War I on the side of Great Britain's enemy, Germany. Prime Minister David Lloyd George was convinced that the defeat of the Turks in Palestine would eliminate Turkey from the war. General Edmund Allenby's victory over the Turks in Palestine—a month before Jerusalem capitulated to the British general—made the Balfour Declaration of November 1917 possible, besides dealing a deathblow to the Ottoman Empire and granting Great Britain administrative rights in Palestine from Jaffa through Jerusalem to Jericho and along the Jordan River to the Dead Sea. By September 1918 Allenby's forces had occupied all of Palestine and Syria with the help of T. E. Lawrence (1888–1935) and the Arab army commander, Emir Faisal. This greatly stimulated Arab nationalism and caused enormous conflicts with new Jewish immigrants to Palestine. A final irony: Already in the nineteenth century the Turks had affirmed Jewish civil rights, while the Balfour Declaration's original purpose was to enlist Jewish support for the Allies in World War I.

☞ A 7.

The first administrator granting patents was Thomas Jefferson. A law passed on April 10, 1790, placed power to grant patents in a board consisting of the secretary of state (Jefferson), the secretary of war, and the attorney general. There was no U.S. Patent Office at the time. It was created by an act passed on July 4, 1836. While Thomas Jefferson was in charge of personally examining all of the applications for patents, he never took out a single patent for any of his own inventions.

☞ A 8.

Having given up farming, fishing, and trapping, the Plains Indians' entire economy centered around the buffalo—for food, robes, tents, even needles from buffalo splinters, thread from buffalo hair, knife handles from buffalo bones, and cups and spoons from buffalo horns. The white man reasoned that once the buffalo was gone,

ANSWERS

the Indians would be that much easier to handle. That was the main reason the buffalo was not protected. In 1830, there were 30 million buffalo in the United States. At the end of the nineteenth century, there were more buffalo living captive in zoos than in the wild, about 2,100 altogether. The Indians had lost the main source of their livelihood.

☞ A 9.

You be the judge: Andrew Jackson had acted in good faith when he married Rachel, the wife of Captain Lewis Robards, in 1791, well before he won the presidential election (1828). Such was the complexity of divorces in the eighteenth century that Captain Robards took advantage of a legislative act passed in December 1790 that allowed him to "sue out" a writ against his wife. When Robards let people know that he had divorced his wife, Jackson married Rachel in August 1791. Only in late 1793 did Jackson learn that Robards had not bothered to file for divorce until the spring of 1793, and a new unconventional marriage bond was issued, dated January 1794, when Jackson most likely married his wife for the second time. Worn out by the unfounded campaign charges of her adultery, Mrs. Jackson died a few days after Andrew Jackson was elected president in 1828.

☞ A 10.

It is far from being a trick question. For about three weeks, a Soviet republic existed in Bavaria, from April 4 to May 1. On that date, it was overthrown by armed forces of the federal government. The year was 1919.

☞ A 11.

Everything is wrong with that statement. Blacks have proven themselves as rightful holders of the franchise as far back as 1853. On July 1, 1853, a constitution was introduced in the Cape Colony, giving each British citizen there (white and black), depending on job and salary, the right to vote for many years. The official policy of apartheid was introduced only in 1947.

☞ A 12.

The two figures represent the former South African prime minister and sometime white supremacist Jan Smuts and the archbishop of Cape Town, Desmond Tutu. However, the visiting public did not get a chance to see the figure of Smuts because it was removed from public view in 1956, long before the rest of the world openly opposed apartheid.

☞ A 13.

Abyssinia, now Ethiopia. Ethiopia's leader, Lieutenant Colonel Mengistu Haile Mariam (b. 1937), claimed after the 1987 election that 96 percent of Ethiopia's electorate of 14 million people took part in the referendum and had approved a constitution providing for civilian Marxist rule.

☞ A 14.

If the president were fully disabled, paralyzed, or hovering between life and death, it would be virtually

ANSWERS

impossible in today's atmosphere of near-total disclosure to have the first lady run the government. More important, the Twenty-fifth Amendment, ratified in 1967, states that the president or the chief of staff in the White House, if the president is too sick to do so himself, shall declare in a letter to Congress that he must hand over his power of the presidency to the vice president and have him discharge the presidential duties. The president can resume his full duties again by writing another declaration of this intent to the Congress of the United States.

☞ A 15.

Members of President Nixon's White House staff actually first contacted J. Edgar Hoover (1895–1972), FBI chief, about raiding offices and working on other covert operations that would help them infiltrate antiwar organizations and eavesdrop on Vietnam war protestors and, in the process, assure Mr. Nixon's reelection. Mr. Hoover was known to be no stranger to electronic bugging and authorized break-ins in the past, but to his credit he had learned to read the mood of the country in the 1960s and he knew that what had been acceptable years earlier to the public and the media would no longer be tolerated at that stage in history. That is why he turned down the White House suggestion to undertake such illegal activities and why members of President Nixon's staff felt they had no alternative but to use the "plumbers"—originally created to plug news leaks—themselves.

☞ A 16.

That was George Kennan's (b. 1904) opinion of Vyacheslav Molotov (1890–1986). Molotov did not even blink

POLITICAL WORLD

when informed by Stalin that his wife had been thrown into jail on Stalin's orders. Her crime: she was Jewish. Molotov continued serving Stalin as faithfully as before.

☞ **A 17.**

True. E. D. Nixon helped to organize the Brotherhood of Sleeping Car Porters, founded by A. Philip Randolph in the 1920s. In 1955, he bailed Rosa Parks out of jail after she was arrested for refusing to yield her seat in the front of a Montgomery, Alabama, bus. E. D. Nixon then enlisted a young man to stage a boycott of Montgomery's blacks, a minister named Martin Luther King, Jr. E. D. Nixon died at the age of eighty-seven in 1987.

☞ **A 18.**

There was no need to introduce such legislation. There were already three amendments, none of which were completely adhered to by some of the U.S. intelligence services. The Tunney Amendment of 1975 prevented covert U.S. operations from attacking Cubans who were consolidating the Marxist MPLA regime in Angola. Then came the Clark Amendment, which scuttled U.S. aid to anti-Communist forces. In the 1980s, the Boland Amendment singled out Nicaragua as the country in which U.S. military help could not be provided to non-Communist contra forces fighting the Marxist Sandinistas.

☞ **A 19.**

More medals were awarded than there were U.S. troops who landed in Grenada in 1984: 8,600 medals for 7,000 troops.

ANSWERS

☞ A 20.

James Garfield (1831–81) in 1880. He was shot by a disappointed office-seeker four months after being inaugurated in March 1881 and died on September 19.

☞ A 21.

Julius Caesar (c. 102–44 B.C.).

☞ A 22.

The member was Edward Dickinson, serving as a representative from Amherst, Massachusetts, from 1853 to 1855. His daughter was the poet Emily Dickinson (1830–86). This relationship is not mentioned in the *Biographical Directory of the American Congress.*

☞ A 23.

Both of them were assistant secretary of the U.S. Navy.

☞ A 24.

The youngster was one of the first babies ever named after the Founding Father: Washington Irving (1783–1859). The Irvings' Scottish maidservant brought this to the attention of the general while the three of them were in a Manhattan shop in 1789, and Washington responded with a pat on the future writer's head. This was mentioned by Irving himself shortly before he died in a biography he was preparing of the first president.

☞ A 25.

Richard M. Nixon.

☞ A 26.

Only one: Andrew Jackson. The last time there was no national deficit or federal debt, a situation that led to the worst depression the republic had yet experienced, was in 1835 to 1836.

☞ A 27.

Ambassador Joseph C. Grew's greatest weakness was that he did not speak Japanese. His wife, Alice, spoke it fluently and frequently served as his interpreter. She was the granddaughter of Commodore Perry. Grew later served as under-secretary of state from 1944 to 1945, and he was an influential career officer in the State Department in the post-World War II era.

☞ A 28.

The United States traded more per year in the 1980s with Ontario than with the rest of Canada or with *any* other nation on earth.

☞ A 29.

1) A major part of borrowed capital was used to over-spend on means of production, for which the borrowers were unable to pay. 2) Burdened with astronomical

reparations, the Germans were compelled to borrow money from American banks (which they knew they could not repay) to pay the British and French as part of their punishment for unleashing World War I on them. 3) Huge amounts of food were imported from Europe in exchange for cash that it was hoped the Europeans would use to buy American-made machinery. This sent about a third of U.S. farmers into bankruptcy because they could not sell their produce.

☞ A 30.

For over three decades, Soviet military personnel were stationed in their own military installations inside Cuba. So were, and are, American military at the U.S. naval base of Guantánamo, which is located on the southeast coast of Cuba.

☞ A 31.

Leslie King was born in Omaha, Nebraska, on July 14, 1913. When he was an infant, his parents were divorced and his mother married Gerald Ford, Sr. Mr. Ford adopted the boy and gave him his name. Otherwise, the United States would have had its first King as president in the White House.

☞ A 32.

The phrase "cold war" was first used in a speech by Bernard Baruch in 1947, but the media also used it in the late 1930s.

POLITICAL WORLD

☞ **A 33.**

The judges and jury at the Barbie trial of 1987 did not weaken at all on the last of the 341 specific questions, determining the unrepentant German war criminal's guilt. The question asked specifically whether there were any mitigating circumstances to excuse Barbie of his responsibility in sending thousands of innocent people to their deaths. To this question, the judges and jury answered no.

☞ **A 34.**

In 1881, there were three American presidents: Rutherford B. Hayes (1822–93); James A. Garfield (1831–81), who died of gunshot wounds inflicted by an assassin; and Chester Alan Arthur (1830–86), who succeeded Garfield. There were also three presidents in 1841: Martin van Buren (1782–1862); William Henry Harrison (1773–1841), and his successor John Tyler (1790–1862), who died of pneumonia after a month in office.

☞ **A 35.**

In 1916, President Wilson thanked Hollywood producer Thomas Ince for his movie *Civilization*. Its pacifist, isolationist message reinforced America's belief that it should stay out of the European war. A year later, however, Americans had become so incensed over the brutality committed by Germany's armed forces, as well as its unrestricted submarine warfare and the interception and disclosure of Germany's Zimmermann Telegram, that it was relatively easy to bring the United States into

World War I on the side of the Allies. As a result, D. W. Griffith's (1875–1948) magnificent, irenic 1916 film *Intolerance* was a financial flop on its first run.

☞ A 36.

The author was Gunnar Myrdal (1898–1987). The book, cited by the U.S. Supreme Court in its 1954 decision, appeared in two massive volumes in 1944 and had a first printing of only 2,500 copies. It was entitled *An American Dilemma.* His wife, Alva Myrdal, who was a co-winner of the 1982 Nobel Peace Prize, died in 1986.

☞ A 37.

The individual states could *not* determine their own policy toward slavery. That is where the northern and western American states differed from the states in the South that had not yet joined the Union. Slavery was strictly prohibited from the outset in any part of the original thirteen states and any state joining the Confederation.

☞ A 38.

1) Alexander Hamilton 2) John Dickinson of Delaware 3) Benjamin Franklin.

☞ A 39.

The Pan-German Nationalist party of Austria was the force behind the anti-Semitic movement. Its founder,

Georg Ritter von Schönerer, a virulent anti-Semite, used the money earned by his father, who was the director of a Rothschild-controlled Austrian railroad company. Schönerer was highly praised by Hitler in *Mein Kampf* as one of the two greatest Austrian political anti-Semitic influences in his early life. The other influence was the anti-Semitic mayor of Vienna, Dr. Karl Lüger.

☞ A 40.

Impellitteri became the first candidate elected mayor of New York without the support of a major political party. He ran and won on the Experience ticket in November 1950.

☞ A 41.

They do not, nor do they give right-wingers easy access and a special welcome. A right-winger and racist who was denied admission on the grounds that it would have been "prejudicial to the public interest" was the prime minister of what used to be Rhodesia, Ian D. Smith (b. 1919). Another right-winger who was excluded by the Reagan administration was El Salvador's far-right leader Roberto d'Aubuisson (1943–92). As a matter of fact, in 1984 only seven people were excluded for political reasons, and in the last twenty years fewer than 500 people were denied admission into the United States out of over 70 million nonimmigration visas.

☞ A 42.

Yes and no. The 1487 act was abolished in 1641 by Charles I, even though the administration of justice by the local courts was so fair and effective that King Henry VII was loved by the majority of his subjects for his judicious moderation and his concentration upon the essentials of governing his people. Francis Bacon described Henry VII as "a wonder for wise men." He is considered the greatest of the Tudor sovereigns, and it was only after the king's death in 1509 that the Star Chamber deteriorated into the inquisitorial juryless court of arbitrary methods with which the term *Star Chamber* is identified today.

☞ A 43.

An aide told Khrushchev that a few hours earlier a U.S. spy plane had violated Soviet air space and been shot down. For a whole week, the Soviets would not disclose this news. Meanwhile, U.S. authorities announced that an unarmed U.S. weather reconnaissance plane taking off from Turkey had not arrived at its destination. After several more official denials that it was an espionage plane, Americans were shocked to learn that the pilot of the U-2 plane, Francis Gary Powers (1929–1977), had been taken prisoner by the Soviets and confessed to being employed by the U.S. government to engage in espionage activities with his powerful aerial cameras over the Soviet Union. One of the results of the disclosure was that the Soviet premier scuttled the Paris summit meeting with President Eisenhower, Great Britain's Prime Minister Macmillan (1894–1986), and France's De Gaulle (1890–1970).

☞ A 44.

The name "public" school originated several centuries ago (Winchester was founded in 1382, Eton in 1440), meaning that the schools would accept not only local students, but those from other parts of the country as well—in other words, from the general public.

☞ A 45.

Henry Ford, Sr., the automobile manufacturer (1863–1947).

☞ A 46.

The president who made the statement and threatened to veto the road bill was Andrew Jackson. The year he made the observation was 1830. Jackson had enough clout to make his veto of the Maysville Road Bill stick.

☞ A 47.

Nobody wrote the speech for Dr. Martin Luther King, Jr., nor did he prepare the speech himself. In fact, he wandered completely off his original text, to the distress of some of those on the platform with him on August 28, 1963, and as he forgot the planned speech he improvised the famous "I have a dream" segment of the Washington address.

☞ A 48.

President Reagan had only one press secretary in the White House: James Brady. After Mr. Brady was severely wounded outside a Washington hotel following an assassination attempt on Mr. Reagan by twenty-five-year-old John W. Hinckley, Jr., the president decreed that Mr. Brady keep the title of press secretary, although he could no longer function in the role, and that his successors be referred to as White House spokesmen.

☞ **A 49.**

Japan and the former Soviet Union. The latter is prepared to sign a peace treaty with Japan, but Japan will not do so until Russia returns four small islands north of Japan that the Soviet Union occupied in the last few days of the war. Russia refuses to return the islands to Japan; consequently no peace treaty will be signed and the two countries still are technically at war. This problem, however, is expected to be resolved in the late 1990s.

☞ **A 50.**

The Pledge of Allegiance was not lifted from any historical document, executive proclamation, or politician's words. The original twenty-two words were drawn up in 1892 by a staff member of the now-defunct Boston magazine *Youth's Companion.* The writer of the draft, Francis Bellamy, was a Christian Socialist who had been ousted as a pastor of a Baptist congregation after being accused of preaching "against the rich." It was only then that Mr. Bellamy was hired by the Boston weekly. In 1925 the words "my flag" were emended to "the flag of the United States" and as late as 1954 Congress added the words "under God" after "one nation." The pledge was originally intended for recital at ceremonies marking the 400th anniversary of Columbus's discovery of America.

☞ A 51.

The statement was made in 1938 after Great Britain's Prime Minister Neville Chamberlain had met with Adolf Hitler and aired his opinion of the Führer.

☞ A 52.

Prime Minister Stanley Baldwin (1867–1947) of Great Britain refused to appoint Winston Churchill as his minister of defense in 1936, claiming that "if I pick Winston, Hitler will be cross." He made the statement after Hitler had invaded the Rhineland.

☞ A 53.

No, it was neither President Reagan nor President Bush. The citation comes from a presidential report to Congress. The year: 1910. The president: William Howard Taft (1857–1930).

☞ A 54.

The presidential candidate of the Surprise party was George Burns's (b. 1896) wife, comedienne Gracie Allen (1906–64). Surprisingly, she won quite a few thousand votes, especially in Oklahoma.

☞ A 55.

No U.S. president ever did so. It is popularly believed that Abraham Lincoln wrote the November 19, 1863,

ANSWERS

Gettysburg Address on the back of an envelope on his way to Gettysburg, Pennsylvania. The truth is that the speech he delivered there, on the occasion of the dedication of the new national cemetery, had been drafted and redrafted by Lincoln at the White House.

☞ **A 56.**

No, it was not Horace Greeley (1811–72) but a little-known editor from Indiana, John Babsone Lane Soule (1815–91). He had an article published in the *Terre Haute Express* in 1851, which contained this sentence: "Go west, young man, and grow up with the country." Only a considerable time later did Horace Greeley come across this article and quote the sentence in an editorial in his New York daily, the *Tribune*. When the saying became famous, it was attributed to Greeley who, in all fairness, reprinted Soule's article to show where he had found the quotation.

PLACES

☞ **A 1.**

John Calvin (1509–64) never renounced his French citizenship. He did not have to, because Geneva was not Swiss at the time he lived. It was an independent city-state until it was annexed by revolutionary France in 1798. Only in 1815, as a result of the Congress of Vienna, did Calvinist Geneva become the last independent city-state to join the Swiss Confederation. Before 1815 Calvin was popularly known not as a Swiss reformer but as a French reformer, which he really is.

☞ **A 2.**

James Angel saw what is known today as Angel Falls, on a branch of the Carrao River—the highest uninterrupted waterfall in the world (3,212 feet). It is nineteen times higher than Niagara Falls. The fall, known by the

ANSWERS

Indians as Cherun-Meru, was first reported by Ernesto Sanchez La Cruz in 1910.

☞ A 3.

The country is Japan. Montana, which has slightly more land area than Japan, has fewer than a million residents. Japan harbors between 125 and 130 million inhabitants.

☞ A 4.

The tourist attraction is Piccadilly, the fashionable street between Hyde Park Corner and Piccadilly Circus. The collars Baker manufactured were called "pickadils," and the house he retired in was named Piccadilly Hall.

☞ A 5.

The capital of Denmark: Copenhagen. The city is located on the eastern coast of the island of Sjaelland (Zealand) and on the northern part of the island of Amager. The two islands on which Copenhagen is built are joined by two modern bridges, the Langebro and the Knippelsbro. Excavations have established that the site of Copenhagen's inner city has been inhabited for about 6,000 years.

☞ A 6.

Jeréz de la Frontera is famed throughout the world for its sherry wine. There are two hundred viniculturists in Jeréz, and the vineyards cover 20,000 acres. They produce enormous quantities of sherry—19 million gallons for the export market alone.

PLACES

☞ **A 7.**

The name *Alhambra* comes from the Arabic word *alhamra,* which means "red." The walls of the fortified palace, indeed, are a rich pink color. It took over a hundred years, in the thirteenth and fourteenth centuries, to construct the palace before it fell into Christian hands in the late fifteenth century.

☞ **A 8.**

King John (1167–1216), the greedy brother of King Richard the Lion-Hearted, sealed the Magna Carta at Runnymede on June 15, 1215. It has frequently been said that this ended the absolute power of English monarchs, handing it to the people. This is not entirely true. The "Great Charter" of English liberties was forced from King John by the barons. It gave legal rights to the barons, not the common people, although gradually, over the centuries, it did benefit them. Runnymede is a meadow about twenty miles west of London, on the south bank of the Thames.

☞ **A 9.**

Columbus, the Italian explorer whose Spanish name was Cristóbal Colón, first landed on the island of El Salvador (named San Salvador by Columbus). He also discovered Cuba and Hispaniola in 1492, as well as Haiti. On his second trip, the following year, he found the island of Puerto Rico, named Boriquén or Borinquén by the Indian inhabitants. Columbus called it San Juan Bautista. He also visited the Virgin Islands, Antigua, and Santa Cruz. In May 1494 he discovered the island of

ANSWERS

Jamaica; the Spaniards named it Sant' Jago. Only on his third attempt, in 1498, did he land on continental America—South America—where he sighted Venezuela. However, it was the neighboring country of Colombia that later named a mountain after him, Pico Cristóbal Colón (5,775 meters). Before the end of August of the same year, he also sighted Tobago, Grenada, and Margarita. Although he made a fourth voyage, landing in Honduras and Jamaica, he never set foot on territory that is today the continental United States.

☞ **A 10.**

In 1677, the monument was the world's highest free-standing column at 202 feet, this equaling the distance from the monument to the site of the Pudding Lane bakery where the fire began. Charles II ordered a Latin inscription on the north panel of the pedestal, accusing the Papists of having started the fire. This inscription was removed in 1830. Up to 1842 half the people who jumped to their deaths from the monument were bakers.

☞ **A 11.**

The head of the image is a monument sculpted in the likeness of Chephren (c. 2800 B.C.), the Egyptian king of the fourth dynasty and the builder of the second pyramid at El Giza (Gizeh, Egypt). He was the brother of Cheops. The monument was built forty-five centuries ago; Pharaoh Thutmose IV had it restored in 1400 B.C. It guards Chephren's (also known as Khafre) pyramid-tomb and is generally known as the Sphinx.

PLACES

☞ **A 12.**

The former English county was called Monmouthshire. When it was administratively attached to Wales, it was renamed Gwent.

☞ **A 13.**

Construction of Durham Cathedral began in 1093, and additions were still made as late as 1500.

☞ **A 14.**

There is little doubt about it: Mexico City, with a projected 28 million inhabitants.

☞ **A 15.**

The number of people living in developing countries is three-fourths of the world's total. And the ratio of those who will live in Asia in the year 2000 is one of every two people on earth.

☞ **A 16.**

For two reasons. Prussia's Frederick the Second had a passion for Gallic styles, and in 1690 his grandfather had brought to Berlin more than 5,000 French Huguenots, who built their houses in the style of their Parisian heritage. The Berliners felt comfortable in those surroundings and continued to build in this style.

☞ **A 17.**

In the western part of Berlin, the American-designed, American-donated Benjamin Franklin Hall (Congress Hall) near the former Berlin Wall is popularly known as the "pregnant oyster" because of its design.

☞ **A 18.**

The Spaniards called the island San Juan Bautista, and later they changed it to Puerto Rico (Rich Port). The name San Juan, however, remained as the name of the capital city.

☞ **A 19.**

Australia.

☞ **A 20.**

According to William Stevenson's *A Man Called Intrepid,* Swedish movie star Greta Garbo (1905–90). She carried messages for British agents, too.

☞ **A 21.**

1) The length of the canal is about fifty miles (81.5 kilometers). The average number of ships going through is around 12,000 per annum. 2) The amount of water flowing into the locks for each ship comes to nearly 52 million gallons, but this water comes neither from the Pacific nor Atlantic. Some of the water is derived from

the dam-created Gatun Lake, which the ships pass through on their route across the isthmus, and the remainder is tapped from another dam-created lake, the nearby Madden Lake. 3) Unfortunately the water can never be used again once it runs into the locks, and after the ships have passed, it is flushed out to sea. 4) The word that does not apply is *pumped.* No water is pumped into the locks. They operate on the simple principle of water running downhill into them.

☞ A 22.

Sooners; it's still a nickname for residents and natives of Oklahoma. There were pioneers who were granted land in the West—around forty acres—but they could only stake out their territory after a specific opening time that had been posted by government officials. Sooners were those future homesteaders who settled on the land of their choice, especially in Oklahoma, *before* the official date the territory was opened to settlement. They arrived *sooner* than those who abided by the law.

☞ A 23.

This Portuguese settlement, Macao (Macau), is not in Portugal but forty miles west of Hong Kong. Fully 75 percent of the residents are Chinese. The streets have official Portuguese names, but they are known only by their Chinese names. On December 20, 1999, Macao will return to Chinese control.

☞ A 24.

It is the Granta—the name the natives of Cambridge frequently give to that part of the River Cam that flows through Cambridge. The town's name was derived from a corruption of the original Grantebrycge or Granta-bridge. Bridges have existed there for over a thousand years, joining the midlands with the land adjoining the fens of the east.

☞ **A 25.**

The shore station and U.S. base: Little America. The region: Antarctica. The naval aviator was Admiral Richard E. Byrd (1888–1957).

☞ **A 26.**

From A.D. 1000 to A.D. 1200, by the Anasazi Indian civi-lization that flourished in New Mexico's Chaco Canyon. The Indians built huge stone-and-adobe apartment buildings that stood five stories high, and the ruins can still be seen today.

☞ **A 27.**

Connolly Str. (Connollystrasse) 31 was the house in which eight Arab guerrillas of the Black September orga-nization killed two members of the Israeli sports team and took nine more athletes hostage during the 1972 Olympic Games in Munich. All of them were murdered by the terrorists later the same day on September 5, 1972, at the military airfield of Fürstenfeldbruck near Munich. Five of the terrorists were killed in a gun battle with German security forces; the other three were cap-tured by the Germans but released the following month when Black September hijacked a Lufthansa Boeing 727 over Zagreb, Yugoslavia. All three guerrillas were tracked down and killed by Israeli agents years later.

PLACES

☞ A 28.

No, it's not in France. The city is in Canada: Montréal. It is Canada's largest port. In addition, the city is built on an island and is the third largest city in Canada.

☞ A 29.

Berlin, Germany. Even during the racist Nazi period, the name of the subway station was never changed. It still exists today in the western part of Berlin—*Onkel Toms Hütte.*

☞ A 30.

The train is called the *Flying Scotsman.* It is an express train that leaves King's Cross, London, for Edinburgh at 10 A.M.—except during World War II, when it left a half hour earlier.

☞ A 31.

A Spanish royal expedition under Pedro de Mendoza founded a settlement on the estuary of the Río de la Plata (River Plate) in 1536, calling it Nuestra Señora Santa María del Buen Aire (Buenos Aires). Lack of food, disease, and attacks from native Indians forced the Spanish colonists to abandon the settlement and move upriver in 1541 to Asunción on the Paraguay River. When this place became overcrowded and subject to opposition from Irala, the new governor confirmed by the Spanish crown, Juan de Garay, left Asunción and moved back to the west bank of the Río de la Plata. He

ANSWERS

planted a permanent Spanish settlement there in 1580, founding Buenos Aires for the second time, thirty-nine years after the original settlers had deserted their colony.

☞ A 32.

A statue that its sculptor, Frédéric Auguste Bartholdi (1834–1904), called "Liberty Enlightening the World." It is better known as the Statue of Liberty and is located in New York Harbor. It arrived in 214 cases on the French steamer *Isère*. While the $250,000 for the statue was contributed by France, the United States raised $350,000 for assembling and soldering the various parts of the statue and erecting its huge granite and concrete pedestal.

☞ A 33.

Poe moved to what is now known as the Bronx. The Edgar Allan Poe Cottage is situated on the Grand Concourse and Kingsbridge Road. His wife, who suffered from tuberculosis, died a year after they moved into this rural wooden cottage, for which Poe paid rent of one hundred dollars a year. In 1913 the cottage was moved across the street into the park created especially for it. The close-by St. John's College is known today as Fordham University.

☞ A 34.

The architect John McComb designed Hamilton's house—Hamilton Grange—which was completed in 1802, in upper Manhattan on 143rd Street. At that time,

PLACES

the neighborhood was still rural, and in 1889 the home was moved two blocks south, to 141st Street and Convent Avenue. The other famous building John McComb is credited with designing is New York's City Hall.

☞ A 35.

The two men were Wilbur (1867–1912) and Orville (1871–1948) Wright, the sons of Bishop Milton Wright of the Church of the United Brethren in Christ. It was over Huffman Prairie that the two brothers first experimented with their gliders and motor-driven airplane. They finally tested the plane in 1903 at Kitty Hawk, North Carolina, where Orville became the first man to make a twelve-second sustained free flight in a motor-driven plane on December 17, 1903, at 10:35 A.M. It reached an altitude of ten feet and traveled through the air for about forty yards.

☞ A 36.

The name of the place, northwest of Stockholm, is Uppsala, known today for its university and as the seat of the Lutheran Archbishop of Sweden. More than a thousand years ago, the Uppsala kings ruled both the Götar and the Svear—the tribes in the north and south of Sweden—and united both of them under one crown and country.

☞ A 37.

The natural product is cork. Actually, the cork is dead bark and can be removed from the oak without killing

ANSWERS

the tree. After the first stripping, however, the cork may be removed from a cork oak only once every nine years.

☞ A 38.

Europe's longest suspension bridge connects Lisbon and Almada in Portugal. It crosses the Tejo River, which in English-speaking countries is called the Tagus.

☞ A 39.

The "White Spider" is a large area on the north face of Eiger Mountain in Switzerland. It is usually swept by avalanches and falling rocks and is avoided by virtually all mountain climbers.

☞ A 40.

The Republic of South Africa. The administrative capital, Pretoria, houses the Union Government Building; Cape Town is the legislative capital, where the houses of parliament are located; and the judicial capital is Bloemfontein.

☞ A 41.

The islands' name: The Galápagos. Galápago is Spanish for tortoise or fresh-water turtle. There are only about 10,000 turtles on the Ecuadoran islands today; they came near extinction over the last hundred years because crews of ships that stopped there killed hundreds of thousands of them for food.

PLACES

☞ **A 42.**

His name was Jean Baptiste Pointe du Sable. He was a black fur trapper and trader who, in 1796, left his trading business in the hands of John Kinzie, who became the first permanent white settler in what is now downtown Chicago.

☞ **A 43.**

The Great Pyramid is made of 2.3 million limestone blocks, each weighing about two-and-a-half tons.

☞ **A 44.**

The most frequently visited museum in the world today is the Georges Pompidou National Center for Art and Culture in Paris, France. On the average it has about seven million visitors a year.

☞ **A 45.**

In Kuwait, prior to the 1991 Persian Gulf War. Only about 7 percent (or 28 percent if native Catalans are included) of the population of Andorra are Andorrans. Andorra is an autonomous coprincipality of the European Community (EC).

☞ **A 46.**

The country is Bolivia.

ANSWERS

☞ **A 47.**

On the moon.

☞ **A 48.**

Articles have been named after these geographical locations. Berlin is a four-wheeled carriage. Wellington is a high leather (sometimes rubber) boot. Winchester is a firearm. Panama is a fine straw hat. Inverness is a full sleeveless cape of wool or worsted in a plaid pattern. Holland is unbleached linen or cotton cloth. Toledo is a specially tempered sword. Hamburg is a rare breed of small European fowl. Hamburg steak is also referred to as a "hamburg."

☞ **A 49.**

The place with the large and small Ferris wheels and roller coasters is Coney Island. Freud loved it.

☞ **A 50.**

Both were the only independent countries in Africa at the time.

☞ **A 51.**

The country is Tibet, which is controlled and occupied by the Chinese Communists. The Potala Palace is the former residence of the Dalai Lama, who lives in exile in India.

PLACES

☞ **A 52.**

His name was Alexandre Gustave Eiffel (1832–1923). He built what was then the tallest structure in the world, the 984-foot-high Eiffel Tower.

☞ **A 53.**

The English name is a corruption of the Dutch "Krom Moerasje." It has become "Gramercy," and the location is Gramercy Park in New York City, the home of Edith Wharton, Herman Melville, Stephen Crane, Carl Van Vechten, and many other celebrities.

☞ **A 54.**

The man honored in this fashion was President James Monroe (1758–1831). The capital is Monrovia, Liberia.

☞ **A 55.**

Mainland China's production of milk, butter, and cheese is virtually nonexistent (just like the biochemical Rh negative factor in the blood cells of the Chinese population). Many Chinese cannot tolerate the lactose in dairy foods. Milk production amounts to about 3 percent of that of Europe, which has over 700 million inhabitants—only about half as many as China.

☞ **A 56.**

The state of Maine does not border on the state of Massachusetts, yet was part of it. Maine was admitted to the union as a state in March 1820.

☞ A 57.

The state is Louisiana, and it was named after Louis XIV (1638–1715), the grandson of the first Bourbon king, who was also known as Henry the Great and Henry of Navarre (1553–1610).

☞ A 58.

Robert D. Emmerich, a pianist and composer who played with the Tommy Dorsey Band, collaborated with Buddy Bernier and Joseph Meyer on a song called "The Big Apple" in the 1940s. Columnist Walter Winchell (1897–1972) liked the song so much that he started calling New York the "Big Apple."

☞ A 59.

In the eighteenth century the now very respectable, exclusive Beacon Hill was referred to as Mount Whoredom. As late as 1817 a minister named it "Satan's seat." Several hundred prostitutes plied their trade there and it had many taverns, until Mayor Josiah Quincy arrested the fiddlers and revoked the liquor licenses. The prostitutes and taverns moved to Ann Street, which is North Street now and was known in the nineteenth century as the "Murder District," since it was lined with "gambling dens, dance halls, bistros, and brothels."

☞ A 60.

Nigeria.

PLACES

☞ A 61.

The place is Anzio. On January 22, 1944, U.S. and British troops landed on its beaches and fought the Germans there, reducing most of Anzio to rubble but paving the way for the Allied liberation of Rome the following June 4. The two emperors were Nero (A.D. 37–68) and Caligula, although in their time Anzio was known as Antium.

☞ A 62.

Less, much less. Only about 1.5 percent.

☞ A 63.

Ekaterinburg was the Siberian town in which the Czar Nicholas II and his family were executed in July 1918. Some historians claim, however, that the imperial family was murdered either in a house formerly belonging to a merchant named Ipatiev or at a nearby abandoned iron mine. The name of the man who gave the order for their execution, on Lenin's instructions, was Yakov Sverdlov, the first Soviet president. In 1991 Sverdlovsk reverted to its original name, Ekaterinburg, sometimes spelled Yekaterinburg.

☞ A 64.

The Mansion House, the official residence of the lord mayor of London.

ANSWERS

☞ **A 65.**

The misquotation can be seen in the Poets' Corner in London's Westminster Abbey. The lines inscribed on the scroll are Prospero's from *The Tempest*. They are slightly out of order. However, Shakespeare (1564–1616) is buried in Stratford-upon-Avon.

☞ **A 66.**

St. John's Church in London's Smith Square, designed by Thomas Archer in 1713 and England's most expensive church at the time. The Luftwaffe gutted the interior during World War II, and the building now functions as a concert hall.

☞ **A 67.**

The bronze Lady of Justice, holding a sword in one hand and the scales of justice in the other, is the highest outdoor statue in London, standing 212 feet (65 meters) above street level. More important, she is the only unhooded figure of Justice on a courthouse in England.

☞ **A 68.**

The highest outdoor statue in London is the Lady of Justice on the Old Bailey's dome, but Lord Nelson's statue is the highest London statue serving as a memorial to an actual person.

PLACES

☞ **A 69.**

If you thought in terms of the 1989–90 mass demonstrations that renounced Communist parties in Eastern Europe and the Soviet Union, and you picked France as the "odd man out," you're wrong. Two of the mentioned countries, for example, did *not* protest in the 1980s and 1990s, but both of them—Austria and France—revolted with the other countries in 1848. The exception (and correct answer) is Czechoslovakia, which was not even established until October 1918 and in 1993 split into two independent republics.

In 1848, though, Prague and Hungary were part of the Habsburg empire and they did demand national rights in June; Vienna had swept Metternich (1773–1859) out of office already in March; and Paris had forced its last Bourbon king to abdicate. Riots for self-determination raged through the Balkans, Berlin, Leipzig, and Poland, and the impoverished masses fought for their rights in parts of Russia. But Czar Nicholas I (1796–1855) and others counterattacked, and by the end of 1849 virtually every liberal victory in Europe had been reversed.

☞ **A 70.**

Both times Polish troops ruled Moscow. On June 20, 1605, Moscow was invaded by a Polish-Lithuanian army and ruled by its commander in chief, known to history as Pseudo-Demetrius I, who was crowned czar on July 21, 1605. This impostor was a Polish protégé claiming to be the son of Ivan the Terrible. (The real Demetrius was killed as a child in 1591.) Pseudo-

ANSWERS

Demetrius I was slain in the Kremlin in 1606 and his army expelled.

In 1610 the Polish army, this time under General Zolkiewski, seized Moscow again. Ladislaus (Wladislaw) IV of Poland was elected czar, but the Muscovites attacked the invader in 1611 and the remnants of the Polish army, including Zolkiewski, took refuge in the Kremlin, where they surrendered in 1612. Then the Russian dynasty, known as the House of Romanov, ruled Russia until 1917.

☞ A 71.

Portugal's Catherine of Braganza (1638–1705), queen consort of Charles II. The place named for her is the New York City borough of Queens.

☞ A 72.

The irony is that this battle—known to history as the Battle of Shiloh—derives its name from a biblical town whose name is the Hebrew word for "sanctuary." The Israelites kept the Ark of the Covenant in the tabernacle there, where the Lord appeared to Samuel (1 Sam. 3–4).

RELIGION

☞ **A 1.**

There were two popes named John XXIII. Both of them were very popular. The twentieth-century pope, familiar to most of us, was John XXIII, who served from 1958 to 1963; he introduced far-reaching reforms and promoted cooperation with other religions. The antipope ruled in Pisa from 1410 to 1415. In fact, he reigned with another antipope, Pope Benedict XIII, stationed in Avignon, while the canonically elected pope was Gregory XII, who sat in Rome. As a matter of fact, there were also two popes named Benedict XIII. One was the antipope in Avignon, ruling from 1394 to 1423, the other the legally elected pope in Rome, Benedict XIII, who ruled from 1724 to 1730.

☞ **A 2.**

The Christian theologian Martin Luther (1483–1546). He wrote this in 1523 in his pamphlet entitled "Jesus Christ Was a Jew."

ANSWERS

☞ **A 3.**

The answer is Martin Luther, near the end of his life.

☞ **A 4.**

Nobody knows for sure what caused the change from his benevolence toward the Jews to his blistering attacks on them in his essays "Concerning the Jews and Their Lies" and "Schem Hamphoras" (1542). Some scholars blame his bitterness on his deteriorating health; others blame it on the fact that his dream of seeing Jews being converted through his new Reformation teachings did not materialize. Another school believes that he was greatly influenced not only by a flurry of anti-Semitism in central Europe, but by those Jews who had converted to Christianity at the time (especially Joseph Pfefferkorn) and who spouted unfounded lies about the Talmud and their former faith in order to be accepted by the Church. The embittered Martin Luther was only too eager to embrace these lies late in his life when some of his followers showed tendencies to convert to Judaism.

☞ **A 5.**

It did not. Because in 1903, Herzl did not speak of Palestine as the new Jewish homeland, but of the highlands of British East Africa (Kenya), temporarily at least. However, he pointed out that it was to serve as a stepping stone to Palestine. Herzl died the following year. The British had in fact offered El Arish and the Sinai desert to the Jews, but London changed its mind in the belief that the Sinai desert could not be made to

RELIGION

bloom. Kenya became its substitute offer, which was turned down by the Zionists.

☞ **A 6.**

The man was the writer Leo Tolstoy (1828–1910). His home, the new mecca, was Yasnaya Polyana. His new message of selfless love and renunciation of service to the State and possession of worldly goods won him the devotion of large masses of people, a devotion that remains unequaled almost a hundred years later.

☞ **A 7.**

The Church in Apostolic days never dealt with the matter of abortion. Later, and well into the sixteenth century, Christianity did not forbid it until the third month after conception. In fact, Saint Thomas Aquinas did not base conception on biological knowledge but on his metaphysical theory of hylomorphism, which stipulates that the soul can only inhabit the form that is capable of receiving it. Aquinas believed that for about eighty days after conception the embryonic shape was not capable of holding the soul, and the Church generally accepted this principle as well until the sixteenth century.

☞ **A 8.**

The man was the German Protestant theologian and pastor, Dr. Martin Niemöller. In 1937, he was arrested at the Hohenzollerndamm Church in Berlin by the Hitler Youth, on orders of the Gestapo, for attacking the Nazi regime and its anti-Jewish laws. One of Hitler's last orders was to have him executed, but he was liberated

ANSWERS

by the Americans. After the war he continued his ministry at his church in Berlin-Dahlem, became one of the world's leading pacifists, and was elected president of the World Council of Churches (1961–68). He died at the age of ninety-two in Wiesbaden, in what was West Germany, in 1984.

☞ **A 9.**

The human mind will accept dogmatism—the positive assertion of belief—unconditionally as an article of faith that has been divinely revealed, but it will do so only if the divine origin from which the assertion emanates has been established in the mind of the beholder as a positive unalterable force revealing absolute truth.

☞ **A 10.**

Dharma, in the Pali language of the Buddhist scriptures, is *dhamma,* a word derived from *dhara,* meaning to hold, to possess—anything that is right, just: a law. In Brahmanism it is interpreted as the cosmic law of Varuna, the god of the heavens. In Buddhism, it has seven meanings, among them an object or appearance; a characteristic; existence in the chain of causation; nirvana; and Buddha's philosophy. In Hinduism, it is the religion-inspired moral ideal that sustains the world and the Eternal Law.

☞ **A 11.**

The French artist was Honoré Daumier (1808–79). Most of his work, including roughly 4,000 lithographs, appeared in the periodical *Charivari.*

RELIGION

☞ A 12.

The Ferrarese ambassador to Rome who was investigating the morals of Lucrezia for her fitness to marry the son of the Ferrarese Duke Ercole gave a most favorable account of Lucrezia to his duke. It is true that Lucrezia's brother, Cesare (1476–1507), had Lucrezia's second husband, Alfonso, killed, but this was an act of revenge for Alfonso's failed assassination attempt on Cesare. Lucrezia forgave her brother but was inconsolable at her husband's death. Rumors among their Neapolitan enemies and the wits of Rome often accused Lucrezia of incestuous relationships with her brother and her father, Pope Alexander VI. But historians specializing in that era are now agreed that these rumors bear no relation to the truth and are only the meat of dramatists. Lucrezia (1480–1519), a linguist and poet, devoted herself to works of charity. She lived with her third husband and was beloved by the people of Ferrara when she died, at age thirty-nine, after giving birth to her (stillborn) seventh child.

☞ A 13.

The main reason for the rumors of defilement is that the Romans did not like the idea of Spaniards occupying the papal throne and readily believed and passed on the rumors sprouting everywhere about the Borgias. Even Pope Alexander's death was attributed to his manipulation of the murder of Cardinal Adriano da Corneto with poison. The truth is that Alexander VI (1431–1503), like many members of the papal Borgia household, died of malaria in August 1503. Cesare, Lucrezia's brother, ended his turbulent life in battle in

ANSWERS

1507. The reason Alexander and Cesare reclaimed the papal states was to suppress the unruly barons who had tried to destroy the Church with territorial wars.

☞ A 14.

The Jews were blamed for the defection of the Reformers, which was ironic because Luther, who had studied Hebrew and later became anti-Semitic, supported the humanist Johann Reuchlin (1455–1522) when the latter defended the Talmud, which interprets the Jewish laws and beliefs, said to be of divine origin. Pope Pius IV (1559–65) terminated all the liberal pro-Jewish policies of the Renaissance popes. Pius IV even allowed sixty Jews to be burned alive in the Inquisition. The Roman ghetto was built and Jews no longer were permitted to own land or enter any profession except the most menial. All synagogues but one were destroyed and communication of any sort with Christians was banned. Many of these measures directed against the Jews were promulgated in Paul IV's bull *Cum Nimis Absurdum* a few years earlier.

☞ A 15.

There was no mass exodus. Only a few Lutherans deserted their church. At the time Sweden was about 95 percent Lutheran; in the 1990s the percentage is down to about 90 percent, with none of the other religious faiths comprising more than 1½ percent each.

☞ A 16.

False. Napoleon I had Pope Pius VII (1742–1823) arrested in Rome on July 6, 1809. He was held prisoner at Savona for three years. After that, in June 1812, he was transferred to Fontainebleau. To an extent, Napoleon regretted his action later; he said that he only removed him to get him away from the bad advice of his cardinals. The truth is that Napoleon could not forgive the pope for having excommunicated him and the French invaders and for Pius's rejection of the proposal that the Papal States become part of France. In 1812, Napoleon brought the Sacred College of Cardinals under his influence and moved it to France. He sincerely believed that God had given him the right to undertake such things.

☞ A 17.

By the mid-1960s, many of Dr. King's followers were no longer loyal to his nonviolent approach to the struggle to gain equality for the minorities. Dr. King spent a large part of his last years opposing U.S. involvement in Vietnam. He became increasingly convinced that nonviolence was a philosophy that should govern relations between nations as well as individuals. This disturbed his traditional supporters, such as Dr. Ralph Bunche, Carl Rowan, Bayard Rustin, and others. They felt that his devoting so much energy to the peace movement would impede black progress in the United States.

☞ A 18.

The Counter-Reformation had not even started yet when Leo X was pope; however, Leo's depleted treasury needed replenishing because in 1520 he depleted the Vatican finances, having paid 20,000 ducats ($250,000) for ten tapestries that he wanted to hang as companions to Michelangelo's ceiling in the Sistine Chapel.

ANSWERS

Raphael (1483–1520) was commissioned in 1515 to do the cartoons, considered to be among the finest drawings ever made, and in Brussels they were transferred to silk and wool. These masterpieces emptied Leo's treasury. Today the tapestries hang in the Vatican's Hall of Arrases. To help defray the expenses of the tapestries, further sale of indulgences and offices was necessary. After Leo's death the tapestries were pawned to ease the papal insolvency.

☞ A 19.

The common strand is metempsychosis, more commonly known as reincarnation.

☞ A 20.

In a 1986 article in the science magazine *Nature,* a trio of biologists suggests that Eve lived between 140,000 and 280,000 years ago in sub-Saharan Africa and that she was the ancestor of *Homo sapiens* on earth today. She wasn't the ancestral mother of all humans; there were other female ancestors of the genus *Homo* living in Africa nearly four million years ago, reproducing even before her, who have modern descendants. But their Eve appears in everyone's genealogy; this conclusion was drawn by studying mitochondrial DNA (mtDNA), which is the DNA outside the cell nucleus and inherited only through the mother. It is easily traced since it never mixes with paternal genes as it is passed from generation to generation. A 1991 study revealed that the greater genetic diversity of living Africans proved that they are the product of the longest evolutionary lineage. At the same time, Dr. Alan Templeton, a geneticist at Washington University in St. Louis, maintained in

RELIGION

a 1992 article in the journal *Science* that scientists may
never resolve the issue of modern human origins and
that one cannot deduct the evolutionary picture of a
species from one strand (mtDNA) of genetic evolution.
Some other molecular biologists agree with the latter
theory, maintaining that the idea of a single place of origin (which definitely does include Africa) can be dis-
puted and that the evolution of modern humans over
200,000 years ago occurred almost simultaneously in
many places due to a climate and flora favorable to the
genus *Homo*.

☞ A 21.

It was Catholicism until 1984 when a concordat was
signed between the Vatican and Italy disclaiming it as
the state religion.

☞ A 22.

The Christian reformer was the English Oxford professor John Wycliffe. He died in 1384—Martin Luther was
born in 1483—and was buried in Lutterworth. Both
Wycliffe and Martin Luther had attacked the corruption
and wealth of the popes and denied papal infallibility.
Wycliffe's remains were dug up almost half a century
after his burial and burned at the command of Pope
Martin V in 1428.

☞ A 23.

The country is Japan. The religion that derives its name
from the language of another country is Shintoism.
Shinto is actually the Chinese name for the "way of the

ANSWERS

good spirits." In Japan, it became known later as *Kamino-Michi,* which also includes smaller related religions (together they account for 39.5 percent of the population). However, the greatest number of followers of a single religion in Japan belong to the school of Buddhism (38.5 percent). The reason why the third sect, Confucianism, has the greatest influence on its adherents is that its tenets include belief in Shintoism as well and its followers may also, simultaneously, be followers of Christianity, Taoism, or Buddhism.

☞ A 24.

Nothing is wrong with the statement, because the Jewish leaders did reply that Jesus Bar-Abbas should receive the pardon. But ever since Jesus of Nazareth had defied the authority of the priests, who tolerated the merchants and money-changers in the inner court of the Temple, they had wanted Jesus of Nazareth to be removed.

☞ A 25.

It *was* a camel. When Mohammed, much like Jesus in Jerusalem, preached against the rich merchants in Mecca who used the Well of Ishmael and the Temple of the Kaaba as sources of profit, and chose twelve men as his Apostles to spread Islam in Yathrib, the leaders and merchants of Mecca tried to kill Mohammed. But the prophet Mohammed just managed to flee from Mecca to Yathrib on his favorite camel, Al Kaswa, who thus saved his life. That escape in A.D. 622 is commemorated now as the most important date in the religion of Islam. Today it is remembered as the *Hegira,* the Night of the Flight.

RELIGION

☞ **A 26.**

Fifty years after the Babylonians conquered the Jews of Palestine and the Kingdom of Judah, the Persians defeated the Babylonians. Persia's King Cyrus (600–529 B.C.) permitted the Jews to return and rebuild their kingdom, in 538 B.C. In gratitude, the Jews studied the Persians' religion—Zoroastrianism—which believed the world to be ruled by two forces: the Good and Wise Lord and the Evil Spirit. The Jews could not conceive of a Creator divided in two and concluded that Jehovah was one God who ruled everything. However, the Jews borrowed from Zoroastrianism and adapted for their own purpose the belief in the afterlife—Heaven and Hell—and the arrival of a Redeemer, not the national hero they had hoped would restore a united Hebrew Kingdom as it had been in the days of David and Solomon but a Messiah based on Zoroastrianism's *Sayoshant,* who would bring peace, justice, and happiness to all living things.

☞ **A 27.**

Mark wrote the first Gospel in a climate of fear around A.D. 70, when the Roman legionnaires of the emperor Vespasian (A.D. 9–79) and his son Titus (A.D. 39–81) put down a four-year rebellion led by a group of Jewish rebels known as the Zealots and destroyed Jerusalem. With Mark's audience amenable to the idea, he wrote his account of Christ's life with the implicit purpose of clearing Christians of any involvement in the Jewish rebellion. Matthew, on the other hand, was so grief-stricken by the sacking of Jerusalem and the destruction of

ANSWERS

Christianity's first historical documents at the hands of the Roman legionnaires that he interpreted those events as a divine retribution for the Jews' rejection of Jesus. John and Luke wrote at a time when the young Christian church was abandoning its roots in Judaism. To be acceptable to the Roman audience, they ignored this historical Jesus who sought to cleanse Israel for the coming of God's kingdom and incorporated an anti-Jewish bias into their accounts of Christ's life.

☞ A 28.

In the nineteenth century, Joseph Smith (1805–44) of New York State claimed to have found a book written on golden plates. This book was revealed to him by the angel Moroni, according to Smith's testimony. He founded the Church of Jesus Christ of Latter-day Saints and called his followers Mormons. Imprisoned in Carthage, Illinois, for destroying a printing press when dissenting Mormons exposed the Mormons' polygamous practices, Joseph Smith and his brother, Hyrum, were shot to death on June 24, 1844, by an anti-Mormon mob.

☞ A 29.

The fact is that Judaism is closer to Islam than to Christianity because of the Muslims' Shariah. The Shariah is the legal code devised during the first two centuries after the prophet Mohammed's death in 632. Both the Shariah of the Muslims and the Talmud of the Jews prescribe specific laws that govern the most ordinary tasks of daily life. Christianity, on the other hand, can be defined essentially as a system of beliefs.

RELIGION

☞ A 30.

Almost everything in the question is false. The Sacred
Temple and the Well of Ishmael in Mecca had been worshiped for centuries before Mohammed's birth there.
Mohammed himself was hated in Mecca for most of his
life for pointing out the wrongs committed by the leaders, priests, and merchants in that city. He had to conquer it by military force before being recognized by its
populace as the Prophet and founder of Islam.

☞ A 31.

The Arabic name of God, "Allah," ended up as the spec-
tators' cry at bullfights, "Olé!"

☞ A 32.

The book is the Muslims' Koran.

☞ A 33.

It is mentioned in the Shariah, the Muslims' handbook
for living the ideal life. For the most part, these laws
derive from the Koran and Mohammed's sayings.

☞ A 34.

All these people have founded their own religious
movements: Russell founded the Jehovah's Witnesses;
Fox, the Society of Friends or Quakers; Ann Lee, the

ANSWERS

Shakers; Margaret and Kate Fox, the Spiritualist Movement; Swedenborg, the Church of the New Jerusalem; William Miller, the Adventists; and Campbell, the Disciples of Christ.

☞ A 35.

Analects and *Five Ching* are 2,500-year-old sacred books based on the teachings of K'ung Fu-tzu, who is better known as Confucius. He eliminated crime in the Chinese province of Lu after being appointed as Minister of Crime. The Chinese philosopher died in 479 B.C.

☞ A 36.

The exception is sinfulness. The other four catastrophes are the Four Horsemen of the Apocalypse. They appeared in Jewish and Christian writings between 220 B.C. and A.D. 350 and were assumed to reveal the ultimate divine purpose.

☞ A 37.

The religion is Islam. The initials stand for *Anno Hegira*, the Year of the Flight. It was in Mohammed's fifty-third year that he fled from those who tried to kill him in Mecca and made his safe getaway to Yathrib, the city whose name was changed later to Medina. The followers of Islam count time from that flight (A.D. 622), because after it Mohammed became the founder of Islam; before it he had been a prophet only.

RELIGION

☞ **A 38.**

The heathen Virgil (70–19 B.C.) leads the reader through Heaven, Purgatory, and Hell in Dante's long poem that was posthumously titled *The Divine Comedy.*

☞ **A 39.**

In Buddhism *The Tree of Wisdom* is a state of mind. A branch of the parent tree under which the Buddha (the Enlightened One) is supposed to have attained perfect knowledge is still being worshiped at the ruined city of Anuradhapura, a capital of the ancient Sinhalese kings, now the north central province of Sri Lanka. It is also supposed to be the oldest tree in existence. Siddhartha himself actually worshiped under the parent bo tree at Gaya in Magadha near the Himalayas. The time when Buddha discovered the First Law of Life is referred to by his followers as *The Sacred Night.*

☞ **A 40.**

The poet was Gerard Manley Hopkins (1844–89). In 1868 he burned all his poems under the misapprehension that writing poetry would not be consistent with a religious vocation. Seven years later the rector of Saint Beuno's Seminary encouraged Hopkins to write a poem about a ship stuck in the sand at the mouth of the Thames. The boat was covered by the incoming tide and five Franciscan nuns drowned on it. The newspaper report had a profound effect on Hopkins. He titled his poem "The Wreck of the Deutschland."

ANSWERS

☞ A 41.

Matthew 2:1–12 never makes any mention that there were *three* wise men—the Magi—just wise men. This legend of their being three in number probably can be traced to the fact that the Magi presented Jesus with three gifts.

☞ A 42.

In the first place, God commanded only Adam not to eat fruit from the tree. More important, God did not choose the apple as the Forbidden Fruit. Nowhere in Genesis is there any mention of an apple. Then why has this fruit been accepted as the Forbidden Fruit? Primarily because the word *apple* derived from the Latin text of the Bible. Genesis 2:17 uses the phrase "the Tree of the Knowledge of Good and Evil" from which no fruit was to be picked, and the Latin for the word *evil* in the text is *malus,* which is also the Latin word for apple—hence the analogy. Interestingly enough, certain Hebrew exegetical traditions variously associated the Forbidden Fruit with the fig and the grape. Michelangelo (1475–1564) actually shows the fruit to be a fig in his Sistine Chapel ceiling.

☞ A 43.

Under the Hyksos pharaohs of Egypt's Sixteenth Dynasty, Egypt referred to the Hebrew tribes as "Asiatics." These nomad tribes had infiltrated the Nile Delta to escape famine in Canaan and Syria. They lived peaceably under the tolerant rule of the Hyksos for hundreds of years. However, the Egyptians under Pharaoh Ramses (Ramesses) II (c. 1304–1225 B.C.) considered the Hebrews (Israelites) aliens and inferior to them and subsequently used them as a pool of manpower and slavery. When Ramses forced them to build the city of Pithom the Hebrews fled into the desert of Sinai, as told in the book of Exodus and recalled annually today by Jews the world over during the celebration of Passover.

☞ **A 44.**

Hardly. It would mean a total of two to three million people, or a column 150 miles long ten abreast. More likely, this number represents the entire population of Israel at some later date. Today it is assumed that during the actual Exodus only those related to the House of Joseph (descendants of Manasseh and Ephraim) were involved in the servitude in Egypt while other Hebrew tribes (then despised as "Asiatics") left Egypt also, but by different routes, crossing the Sinai peninsula into Canaan. Collectively, this tragic experience is referred to as the Exodus.

☞ **A 45.**

In 213 B.C. in the province of Ch'in (Ts'in), Shi Huang-ti (259–210 B.C.) ordered the burning of all the works of Confucius (K'ung Fu-tzu) (551–479 B.C.), Mencius (Meng-tzu) (327–289 B.C.), and others in order to make the province's version of history the accepted one. Shi was Ch'in's king and later became the first emperor of a united China. It is from Ch'in that the name of China derived. However, followers of Confucius and other spiritual masters stole copies of their books—written on bamboo slips two feet long—and hid them inside walls. The Ch'in dynasty lasted for only fourteen years and the next dynasty, the Han, soon revived Confucianism.

INDEX

INDEX

INDEX

INDEX

INDEX

INDEX

INDEX

INDEX

INDEX

INDEX

Molotov, Vyacheslav, 226–27
Monitor (ship), 4, 112
Monotheism, 104, 269
Monroe, James, 253
Montalembert, Count of, 113
Montana, 83, 240
Montreal, Canada, 247
Moon, 74, 172, 252
Mormons, 270
Moroni, 105, 270
Moscow, Russia, 97, 257
Müller, Heinrich, 181, 182
Museums, 92, 251
Music, 42, 59, 171, 185, 201
Mussolini, Benito, 54, 191
  campaign against Abyssinia by, 56, 193–94
Myrdal, Alva, 232
Myrdal, Gunnar, 232

Nagasaki, Japan, 9, 119–20, 215
Napoleon I (Bonaparte) of France
  abdication of, 12, 124
  battles of, 36, 161
  battles of, against Russia, 6, 8, 115–16, 118–19, 143–44
  charisma of, 32, 155
  in Italy, 264–65
Nast, Thomas, 136
National Archives of United States, 40
Native Americans, 29–30, 70, 86, 118, 223–24, 246
Naujocks, Alfred, 181–82
Naval battles
  Civil War, 4, 112
  Napoleonic, 161
Nazis. *See also* Hitler, Adolf
  aircraft and airwar of, 58, 67, 198–99
  anthem of, 59, 201
  Austria and, 65, 211–12
  executions of, 63, 67, 209, 218
  gold and treasures confiscated by, 50, 183

Holocaust and extermination policies of (*see* Holocaust, World War II)
  intelligence operations of, 52, 187–88, 198–99
  last governmental center of, 68, 218–19
  noteworthy, 55, 57, 59–60, 61, 67, 148, 191–92, 195–96, 202, 206, 211
  rocket scientists, 184–85, 192
  salute, 59, 202
  sports teams of, 65, 212–13
  trials of, 34, 75–76, 231
  U-boats, 52, 187, 198
Nebe, Artur, 67, 218
Nelson, Horatio, 97, 161, 256
Nero, Roman emperor, 161, 255
Netherlands, Nazis in, 56, 60, 61, 194–95, 203–4, 205–6
New Jersey, 5, 156
Newton, Isaac, 88
New York City, 77, 95, 117–18, 95, 233, 248, 253, 254, 258
New York Times (newspaper), 43–44, 174
Nicaraguan contra movement, 22–23, 73, 140–41, 227
Nicholas II of Russia, 25, 144, 255
Niemöller, Martin, 261–62
Nietzsche, Friedrich, 188
Nietzsche-Förster, Elisabeth, 188
Nigeria, 254
Nile, Battle of, 161
Nixon, E. D., 72, 227
Nixon, Richard M., 35, 114, 159–60, 167, 226, 229
Nobel Peace Prize, 7, 118
Non-Intercourse Act of 1809, 6, 116
Normandie (ship), 4
North Carolina, 90, 249
Northwest Ordinance of 1787, 76–77, 232
Norway, Nazis in, 56, 194–95, 207

INDEX

INDEX

INDEX

INDEX

INDEX